D0139397

Learning Together
Through Inquiry

Learning Together Through Inquiry

From Columbus to Integrated Curriculum

Kathy G. Short,
Jean Schroeder,
Julie Laird,
Gloria Kauffman,
Margaret J. Ferguson, &
Kathleen Marie Crawford

Stenhouse Publishers
Portland, Maine

Stenhouse Publishers

Copyright © 1996 Kathy G. Short, Jean Schroeder, Julie
Laird, Gloria Kauffman, Margaret J. Ferguson, and Kathleen
Marie Crawford

All rights reserved. No part of this publication may be
reproduced or transmitted in any form or by any means,
electronic or mechanical, including photocopy, or any
information storage and retrieval system, without permission
from the publisher.

Every effort has been made to contact copyright holders and
students for permission to reproduce borrowed material. We
regret any oversights that may have occurred and will be
pleased to rectify them in subsequent reprints of the work.

Library of Congress Cataloging-in-Publication Data

Learning together through inquiry : from Columbus to integrated
    curriculum / Kathy G. Short ... [et al.].
        p.   cm.
    Includes bibliographical references (p. 207).
    ISBN 1-57110-033-4 (alk. paper)
    1. Questioning. 2. Inquiry (Theory of knowledge). 3. Elementary
school teaching. 4. Education, Elementary—Curricula. I. Short,
Kathy Gnagey.
LB1027.44.L43 1996
371.3'9—dc20   95-52505
                                                          CIP

Cover and interior design by Joyce C. Weston
Cover and interior photos by the authors
Typeset by Octal Publishing, Inc.

Manufactured in the United States of America
on acid-free paper

05 04   9 8 7 6

Contents

Acknowledgments

As with any long-term endeavor, there are many people who supported us both professionally and personally as we worked, thought, and wrote together. We want to acknowledge the University of Arizona Columbus Quincentenary Program, which provided us with a grant for our initial teacher research. Administrators within Tucson Unified School District gave their support to our research and curriculum development. Colleagues in the Department of Language, Reading and Culture at the University of Arizona have been a strong influence in our professional lives and a continual source of both support and challenge to our thinking. When we needed someone to listen and respond to the many drafts that eventually led to this book, colleagues in our schools and at the university were always there. Others supported us in various ways. LaFon Phillips lent her skills as a photographer. Three student teachers, Diane Coleman-Fields, Ann Biggins, and Monica Gelfond, were part of our group the first year and met with us every other week as we tried to figure out what an inquiry curriculum might look like. We also want to thank friends and family who picked up extra responsibilities so that we would have time to meet and to write, especially the caretaker of the "Short Resort," who kept us supplied with soda and scenic views. Most of all, however, we want to acknowledge the collaboration of the students in our classrooms, who thought with us about inquiry and who constantly challenged us through their reflective insights and their sense of wonder about the world.

About the Authors

Kathy G. Short is an Associate Professor in the Department of Language, Reading and Culture at the University of Arizona. She teaches and researches in the areas of children's literature, curriculum, collaborative learning environments, and inquiry.

Jean Schroeder taught a multi-age primary class at Cragin Elementary School in Tucson. After working full-time on her doctoral program in children's literature at the University of Arizona, she returned to teaching in Tucson Unified School District. She continues to work with teachers and students with special interests in reflective teaching and curriculum.

Julie Laird previously taught half-time kindergarten and half-time Reading Recovery at Cragin Elementary School in Tucson Unified School District. She followed her class on to first grade, but presently she is teaching full-day kindergarten at Van Horne Elementary School in the same district. She continues to do teacher research with a focus on how children learn literacy through play.

Gloria Kauffman teaches at Maldonado Elementary School in a diverse working-class neighborhood in the southwestern part of Tucson. During the research year, she moved with her fourth-grade class into fifth grade. Presently her intermediate multi-age class continues to explore inquiry through the negotiation of curriculum.

Margaret J. Ferguson teaches at Corbett Elementary School in Tucson Unified School District. During the research year, she taught first grade. She has since taught in a multi-age primary classroom (ages six through eight) and has taken her students on to third grade. She continues teacher research looking at multi-age contexts, inquiry, and portfolios as tools to negotiate curriculum.

Kathleen Marie Crawford was a teacher in Tucson Unified School District where she taught both primary and intermediate-aged students. Following this collaborative study she conducted a teacher research dissertation on curriculum negotiation in an inquiry-based classroom. She is currently an Assistant Professor in the Department of Curriculum and Instruction at Illinois State University where she teaches courses in teacher research and literacy.

1 Does Inquiry Make a Difference?
Examining Our Beliefs
About Curriculum

IN OUR LIVES both inside and outside of schools, we are constantly reminded of the power of story (Rosen 1984). When we get together for professional or social reasons, we always tell stories about our recent experiences. In fact, we have reserved the first half hour of our meetings for "storying" before discussing business, and we often stop to tell stories during our conversations. We've found that if we don't take time for stories, we have difficulty completing the tasks we have set for ourselves. Through these stories, we struggle to make sense of our lives as teachers and learners, the kinds of classroom learning environments we are creating, and our students' lives as learners and thinkers.

The stories in this book center on our attempt to understand curriculum as inquiry (Harste 1992). They grew out of questions we were asking about children's understandings and the kinds of learning environments that would support deep, complex learning. To examine our questions, we formed a teacher research group we thought would last for a year. Four years later, we are still meeting and talking. Our group consists of Kathleen Crawford, Margaret J. Ferguson, Gloria Kauffman, Julie Laird, and Jean Schroeder, who are all classroom teachers in elementary schools in Tucson, and Kathy Short, who teaches at the University of Arizona. While we have changed grade levels and schools and moved into and out of graduate coursework, we have continued to meet and think together about curriculum as inquiry.

In examining our initial questions about children's understandings, we came to realize that we needed to make major changes in the kind of learning environments we were creating with the students in our classrooms. These changes involved our thinking about curriculum as inquiry and exploring curricular structures that support inquiry, such as broad concepts and the inquiry cycle (Short and Harste, with Burke 1996).

Exploring Our Tensions as Teachers and Learners

All of us had used writing workshops, literature circles, thematic units, and self-evaluation in our classrooms. We were considered innovative teachers who put time and thought into our teaching and were willing to constantly explore new ideas. We were kidwatchers (Y. Goodman 1978), observing and listening to the students in our classrooms. We made sure that our curricula were carefully developed from students' needs and interests, and we gave students many choices in their learning. They were actively involved in meaningful learning experiences and encouraged to reflect on those experiences through self-evaluation.

While we felt positive about many aspects of our teaching, as learners we paid attention to the tensions we felt in our curriculum and our interactions with children. One such tension was that we had two parallel curricular frameworks: the authoring cycle for reading and writing, and thematic units for content area learning. We were uncomfortable with this separation of content and process. We also began to worry that our thematic units remained teacher directed and that students often seemed simply to gather facts about topics rather than engage in thoughtful investigation of questions and issues. When we started hearing the term "inquiry" at professional conferences, we initially assumed that inquiry was a slightly different version of a thematic unit, but nothing substantially different. However, the tensions we were feeling led us to wonder whether inquiry might offer another approach to curriculum.

Through a summer course on integrating literature into inquiry, we became interested in children's multicultural and historical understandings and came together as teacher researchers to explore children's understandings in our own contexts. In order to study our questions, we realized that we had to create more powerful learning environments in our classrooms to support children as thinkers and learners. As we struggled to create these environments, we began to envision a different curriculum—one based in inquiry.

While many educators were talking about inquiry, we found little in the professional literature on actual classrooms grounded in inquiry. We had come to believe that inquiry offered a different perspective on curriculum, but most of the practical examples we found were updated versions of thematic units. We needed a way to connect our beliefs to practice.

We thought we understood inquiry at a theoretical level, but it wasn't until we tried to live inquiry in our classrooms that we realized that this approach involved a major theoretical shift for us as teachers (Short and Burke 1996). It was difficult to make this shift, and readers of this book will find that our classrooms are in transition from thematic units to inquiry. Taking an inquiry perspective on curriculum was much more difficult than adding another activity or changing the format of our units. It meant a different way of thinking about curriculum. We used many of the same activities and materials as before, but our thinking about those activities and materials had to shift. It was easy to slide back into our old ways of operating in the classroom because this new way of thinking was hard. In addition, when we first moved into this new way of teaching, we had not explored all of the implications or fully experienced a classroom based in inquiry. Sometimes our struggles were rewarded with major break-throughs; other times we just had to keep believing that our struggles would eventually get us some place.

We believe that curriculum is determined through a collaborative process in which both students and teachers have a voice (Dewey 1938). We didn't want to impose curriculum onto children, but we also didn't believe in silencing our voices through a laissez-faire approach. Curriculum is most powerful when teachers, with their experiences, interests, and knowledge (including state and district curriculum mandates), and students, with their experiences, interests, and knowledge, come together. Curriculum developed this way goes beyond what any one individual can produce.

We knew that within this curriculum development process we, as teachers, had the primary responsibility for creating productive learning environments that could potentially raise issues and problems for our specific students (Dewey 1938). We also knew that students needed to be actively and reflectively involved in curriculum as collaborative decision makers about the focus of class inquiries and the questions they wanted to pursue in personal inquiries. The issue for us was finding a way to balance teacher and student voices in this process. We constantly struggled with defining our role as teachers and with finding ways to involve students meaningfully in the process. Our questions and issues about the roles of teachers and students and the mistakes we made are integrated through-out our stories.

We felt the need for structures that would connect classroom inquiries across the year. We became increasingly excited about the potential we saw for broad, umbrella concepts, such as Change, Discovery, Harmony, Bridges, and Sense of Place, to provide connections across different class and personal inquiries. Such concepts allow for examination of almost any topic or issue so there is no limit on what students can decide to pursue. We found that using the concept of Discovery in our classrooms supported our thinking and planning as teachers, gave us a place to start the school year with students, and became a point of connection that each class could weave through personal and group inquiries.

Our teacher research group was essential in helping us work through these many issues about curriculum, inquiry, and roles. We could bring our questions and feelings of discomfort and frustration to the group and know that others would listen and talk with us. We met biweekly in the spring and several times over the summer to make initial plans for the research and the curriculum. We then met biweekly throughout the school year to talk about curriculum and to compare notes on what was and was not working in our classrooms. The following summer and school year, we met once or twice a month to write histories of what occurred in each classroom and to analyze dialogue from the literature circles and interviews with children. We have continued to meet once a month for the last two years to pull together our experiences and write about them in ways that make sense to other educators. This book grew out of many drafts of chapters that we shared with each other to make sense of our experiences.

In the remainder of this chapter, we focus on the theoretical beliefs about inquiry that underlie the classroom stories we will tell in subsequent chapters. Our experiences in moving from textbook teaching to thematic units to inquiry involved a close examination of our beliefs about content areas and learning, and this, in turn, affected our actions in the classroom.

Examining Our Beliefs About Content Areas and Learning

When we were students, content area classes, such as social studies and science, focused on the memorization of specific facts and concepts. We listened to lectures, read textbooks, filled out worksheets, gave "right" answers in class discussions, and took tests about facts, dates, and events that we forgot as soon as the test was over. When we were asked to research a topic, we copied information on assigned topics from the encyclopedia into a "nice" booklet that we handed in to the teacher. We spent a lot of time "covering" many topics and facts and ended up with only superficial knowledge about, or interest in, those topics. Once we were "done" with a topic, we bitterly complained if a teacher returned to it at another grade level.

Early in our teaching experiences, along with many other teachers, we moved from textbook-dominated approaches to thematic units. Instead of textbooks, our students read fiction and nonfiction and engaged in a wide range of activities related to those books and the science and social studies topics we were studying. Students were encouraged to share both what they knew on a particular topic and what they wanted to know. They were involved in problem-solving as they researched topics and prepared projects to share with classmates. In the thematic units, we moved from teaching facts to creating a wide range of activites related to a topic. Sometimes these activities were developed to teach particular facts or concepts, and sometimes they were just a way to have fun with the topic. Our students became more engaged as learners and enjoyed the active involvement. Both we and our students were having more fun.

But then, tensions began to arise. Our units were more exciting, but we realized we were still "covering" topics and supplying information, just as we had before; the only difference was that now we were doing it in more interesting ways. We felt as though we were in an endless cycle of creating activity after activity and that we often engaged in these activities at the expense of critical and in-depth thinking. Children continued to focus on facts; now they gathered facts instead of memorizing them. We were overrelying on books: students were still primarily reading about, not doing, science and social studies.

The topics of our units were frequently trite, with forced connections. At the end of a two-week unit on kites, for example, none of us wanted to hear about kites again. Doing math computations on kite shapes and spelling kite-related words didn't seem especially meaningful. Even more troubling were student comments that indicated they considered themselves "done" with this topic; they had studied it, it was over. Dewey (1938) argues that what makes an experience educative, as opposed to miseducative, is whether conditions are created for further growth in either the same or new directions. Even though students were having more fun in school, we wondered whether they were engaged in experiences that were challenging them to continue learning and growing over time. We were concerned whether students were operating within their zones of proximal development (Vygotsky 1978)—whether they were being challenged to go beyond what they already could do independently to what they could accomplish with some support from other learners.

Gradually, we realized that our move to thematic units had not involved a theoretical shift from the textbook model of curriculum. We, as teachers, were still the ones in charge. We assumed that students would discover what others already knew about a given topic and that we just needed to set up activities so they could do so. Because we developed the units, students were limited by our own knowledge of the topic; the class stayed safely within what we already knew. Our units continued to be based in a deficit model of learning, a focus on what children didn't know. We assumed they would go from being more confused to less confused about the topic.

We spent many hours developing activities and gathering materials for units. Because the creativity came from us, we were exhausted. Eventually we realized that all we had done was move from an isolated curriculum to a correlated curriculum, not to true integration. The activities were correlated to each other because they related to the same topic, but they weren't integrated in powerful ways to support inquiry. Because knowledge was still compartmentalized by activity and by subject area, students still operated within the same limited understandings about content areas that had led us to move away from textbook approaches in the first place (Altwerger and Flores 1994).

Inquiry as Problem-Posing and Problem-Solving Processes

These tensions led us to think more about curriculum as inquiry. We realized that one of the problems with textbook approaches and our thematic units was that they were models of how to *teach* content, not of how people actually inquire about something they want to *understand*. We needed to look at how learners actually pursue inquiry in their lives outside of school. Reading and writing instruction in schools changed dramatically when Ken Goodman (1967) looked at what readers actually do during the reading process and Donald Graves (1983) observed writers engaged in the process of writing. Instead of beginning with questions of how to teach reading and writing, they examined what readers and writers actually do and then thought about what this might mean for classrooms.

As we looked at young children, we were impressed with their lives as inquirers. They live in a constant state of curiosity and learning. For them, inquiry comes from exploring and being interested in the world. Through their active explorations of their world, tensions arise which lead them to ask questions about aspects of the world that puzzle them. They systematically investigate those questions, thereby creating new understandings and new questions and issues (Short and Burke 1991). As we thought about our own experiences, we realized that we spend at least as much of our time exploring broadly and trying to figure out our questions as we do actually researching those questions. Sometimes we couldn't determine our question until we had done the research. Other times, we explored for long periods of time before we could put our feelings of tension into words so that we could focus on that question through further inquiry.

Paulo Freire (1985) argues that inquirers need to be problem-posers, not just problem-solvers. We saw that in our classrooms we were the problem-posers; our students were forced to become the problem-solvers, answering our questions. We realized that problem-solving and research are empty processes when the question is not one that really matters in the life of the inquirer. While there are many research strategies that support our lives as inquirers, focusing on learning those strategies is a waste of time if we don't first take time to find a significant question. Even then, we may not find a specific question, but an interest, an issue, or a general wondering that we want to pursue further. As we work through inquiry, we do not usually end with one answer or even a set of answers. Inquiry does not narrow our perspective; it gives us more understandings, questions, and possibilities than when we started. Inquiry isn't just asking and answering a question. It involves searching for significant questions and figuring out how to explore those questions from many perspectives.

Progress in inquiry is finding new understandings and new questions. The term *understandings* highlights the temporal nature of what we learn, while the term *answers* signals that what we learn from one experience will never change. Carolyn Burke argues that understandings last only until learners have time to ask new questions or create more compelling theories. We don't inquire to eliminate alternatives but to find more functional understandings—to create diversity, broaden our thinking, and ask more complex questions (Short and Burke 1991). We can end up *more* confused, not less confused, but our confusion reflects new questions that are more complex and based on deeper insights.

Teachers do not know exactly what children will learn when they begin a focused study in the classroom because the questions are not framed ahead by teachers and experts. Children have to participate in creating the questions. John Dewey (1938) states that teachers have a responsibility to establish classroom learning environments and select experiences that have the most *potential* for raising anomalies and questions for a specific group of students. They cannot, however, determine exactly what those anomalies will be for students; if they do, they become the problem-posers.

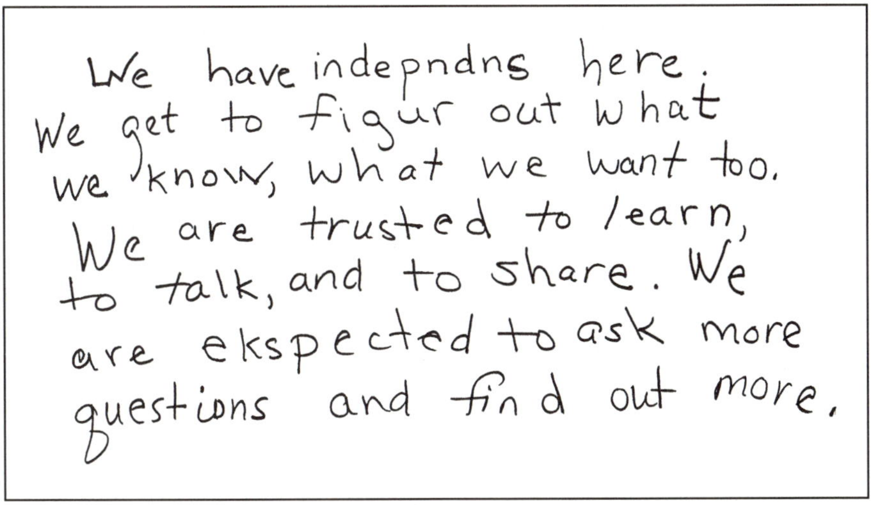
We have indepndns here. We get to figur out what we know, what we want too. We are trusted to learn, to talk, and to share. We are ekspected to ask more questions and find out more.

Figure 1.1
Reflection Log (Amber, Age 11)

Curriculum as Inquiry

Three sources of knowledge are essential to inquirers in their search for significant questions and their investigation of those questions (Harste 1992): personal and social knowing, which is acquired through our life experiences; knowledge systems, which provide structures for organizing knowledge and offer alternative perspectives on our world (e.g., history, biology, psychology); and sign systems, which provide alternative ways of making and creating meaning about the world (art, music, movement, language, and mathematics). Knowledge systems and sign systems are not reduced to subject areas and the mastery of specific facts, procedures, and skills. They are seen as perspectives, ways of thinking, and stances one can take in the world (Short and Harste, with Burke 1996).

The concept of knowledge systems does not involve dividing knowledge into separate areas and learning facts for each of these areas. Rather, knowledge systems offer alternative perspectives on the same topic and diverse strategies and tools for researching that topic. Instead of focusing on how to "cover" the content of subject areas, the emphasis is on pursuing significant questions through using questions and ways of researching from a range of knowledge systems. A conversation with Joan Irwin, a historian from Winnipeg, helped us understand how history could be seen as a knowledge system rather than a collection of facts about events and people. She pointed out that she approaches any situation with the question "How can I use the past to understand the present and to change the future?" She also noted that historians have particular processes and tools for research. These include conducting interviews, taking notes, examining primary sources, and constructing time lines. When children read only textbooks or historical fiction when studying history, they encounter the work of someone else who has engaged in historical research, but are not learning how to engage in that process themselves.

By bringing multiple knowledge systems to a topic, students are able to ask different questions about that topic from the perspectives that each system offers and can choose from a wide range of research processes and tools. For example, when an inquiry group in Jean's classroom became interested in bugs, they first took a historical perspective as they asked, "Who was the first person to discover bugs? What is the history of bugs?" They then moved into a paleontology perspective, where they explored "fly bones," and from there went to a scientific perspective, where they learned that flies have no bones. Finally, they moved to an agriculturalist perspective and asked, "Why do we have bugs? What are they useful for?" Each shift involved new questions, research processes, and tools.

Outside of school, learners do not use only reading and writing to create and share meaning. They have multiple sign systems available, including music, art, mathematics, movement, and drama as well as language (Eisner 1994). Any of these sign systems can be vehicles for learning and thinking about a particular inquiry or for sharing that inquiry. Sign systems allow learners to explore and create new ideas and to share what they are learning as they examine a topic through their own personal experiences and different knowledge systems.

Learners will not pursue the questions that really matter in their lives unless they are in an environment where their ideas and lives are valued (Edelsky 1994). The learning environments that are most supportive for inquiry are those that move beyond hierarchy toward a democracy where all are equally valued. Pat Shannon (1993) defines a democracy as a system in which people participate meaningfully in the decisions that affect their lives. It involves participation and negotiation among equals. Participants are not just given a choice among options determined by others behind the scenes; they are part of the thinking behind the scenes.

As Figure 1.2 illustrates, the smallest unit of curriculum is therefore inquiry itself, not a fact or an activity. Inquiry is a whole process that cuts across and integrates personal and social knowing, knowledge systems, and sign systems within an environment based on education for democracy.

Instructionally, curriculum as inquiry means that instead of using the theme as an excuse to teach science, social studies, mathematics, reading, and writing, these knowledge systems and sign systems become tools for inquiry—for exploring, finding, and researching students' own questions. Curriculum does not focus on activities and books, but on inquiry. Literature comes into this process as it supports inquiry, not as the focal point.

The shift from textbooks to thematic units involved a major change in how our classrooms looked. Many more materials and lots of teacher time were needed to gather books and plan activities. Instead of students sitting quietly at desks, they moved around the room, engaged in a wide range of activities.

The shift from thematic units to curriculum as inquiry is a much more subtle shift because the classroom does not look different on the surface—the same materials and activities are often there. But many of these materials are now gathered by the entire classroom community, not just the teacher; and students set up and create their own sites for exploration instead of only engaging in our preplanned activities. The major difference, however, is in the beliefs underlying those materials and activities and the functions they serve (Short and Burke 1996). This has been a much more difficult change for us as teachers to make. It is easier to change the look of our classrooms than to change how we think about curriculum. We found it especially difficult to move away from the subject areas as the center of the curriculum because schools are organized around this assumption. We often found ourselves still using these areas to organize the curriculum instead of using them as tools to support inquiry.

Figure 1.2
Curriculum as
Inquiry (Short 1993)

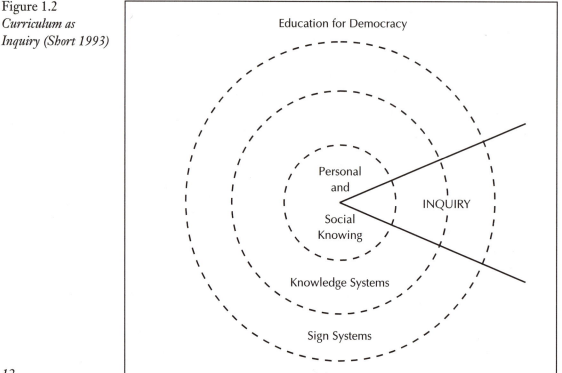

An example of this change in thinking is the difference between Kathy's experiences in Indiana teaching a first-grade thematic unit on the ocean and Kathleen's experiences in Tucson with first and second graders exploring the ocean. Kathy chose the ocean because it was a high-interest topic for first graders and she had many appropriate books and materials to use as resources. At the beginning of the year, she made a list of the units to be studied that year and decided when they would be taught. The ocean was slated for January because she thought it might enliven the Indiana winter. In teaching this unit, she read picture books to the students, pulled together thematic sets of books for browsing in the classroom, and engaged students in activities, such as science experiments with salt water and art activities with watercolor washes and a large mural of sea creatures. She arranged to show movies on the ocean, brought in her own collection of seashells and specimens, and planned learning centers where students categorized seashells and wrote in fish-shaped books. To conclude the unit, Kathy asked students each to choose one sea creature for research and then to write a short informational book with many pictures. At the end of the unit, Kathy gathered up and returned the library books and boxed up her materials until the next January.

In contrast, Kathleen's class inquiry, or focus, on the ocean began when several children went to San Diego over spring break and returned to the classroom with stories about a huge body of water and sea animals that seemed improbable to children who had spent their lives in the desert. The children's questions and interest led to a class decision to study the ocean. Kathleen gathered fiction, nonfiction, and poetry on the ocean from the library as well as a collection of seashells, photographs, art prints, and music. Children who had been to the ocean added their own seashell collections, pictures, and books. Over the course of a week, children had time to tell their stories, browse the materials, and gather each day to share their observations and questions, which were listed on a large sheet of paper. The class then used this list to create a web of questions that were most significant to them. The web became a sign-up sheet for research groups on why oceans have waves, the differences between mollusks and jellyfish, the teeth and jaw structures of sharks, and how to keep ocean water clean. Kathleen and the students pulled together resource sets for each group, and students met in their groups to pursue their research. As they worked, they realized that they needed tools for keeping track of what they were finding, so each group developed some kind of chart, web, graph, or diagram to record their data. Students shared their research through presentations that ranged from murals to written books to dramas. After the class focus ended, many of the books remained in a corner of the classroom, and some children continued their explorations of the ocean throughout the rest of the school year. As they explored the ocean, many students became interested in environmental issues, so the class decided that this topic would be their next class focus.

Many of the same materials, activities, and books were part of both Kathleen's and Kathy's studies of the ocean, but they were used in very different ways. In the thematic unit, Kathy determined the sequence of activities and took the class through the books and activities together as a class. She determined the topics for the research; students were only given the choice of which sea creature to focus on. In Kathleen's classroom, the books and activities supported students as they broadly explored the ocean and found their own connections and questions. Many of the engagements that Kathy used for whole-class activities Kathleen used as exploration centers that children browsed as they wished or used as part of their research group. Kathleen did not assume that all children needed to have the same experiences. Because she gave her students time to explore and to develop their own questions, their research groups reflected a much wider range of topics, which children explored at both factual and conceptual levels. Kathy's students contented themselves with gathering a few facts on their animals to put into their books.

Kathy planned her unit by listing subject areas and then developing activities for each one. She carefully selected activities that drew from science, social studies, mathematics, art, reading, writing, and music. Some were selected because she felt the children would enjoy the activity, while other activities were selected to teach skills from these subject areas. Kathleen also gathered many resources, books, and artifacts. She thought about possible engagements that would allow children to first connect to their own experiences and then explore the ocean from many different perspectives in order to find questions they wanted to pursue through inquiry. She was aware of the importance of different perspectives and so made sure that the resources she brought into the classroom reflected a range of perspectives on the ocean, such as environmentalist, scientific, social, recreational, and literary. These knowledge system perspectives were also highlighted during class discussions. Photographs, paintings, and music about the ocean were part of the resources that children used to learn. They were encouraged to sketch as well as take notes as they read and observed. When they presented their research, they constructed their understandings in the sign systems that best communicated what they had learned. Knowledge systems and sign systems were tools Kathleen's students used to learn about the ocean.

We could see the theoretical and practical differences between thematic units and inquiry when we looked back on our experiences. However, it was not as easy to make these distinctions when we were in the middle of struggling with curriculum in our classrooms. Negotiating a class focus and then finding time to explore that focus and find questions for inquiry was a much more complicated process than we had ever imagined.

Pursuing Individual Inquiries

Most of the classroom examples we share in this book are based on children's inquiries within a class focus. We believe in having a class focus because of the depth of inquiry that is possible when students think together within rich supportive contexts. Within this class focus, students pursue individual and small-group inquiries with support from whole-class experiences and from other learners in the classroom.

However, we also know that students have personal agendas and inquiries that they need to pursue. We worried about how to find a place in our crowded classroom schedules for both a class focus and personal inquiries. Writing work time and wide independent reading were two parts of the school day not directly tied to the class focus. Students could choose to bring that focus into these times, but they did not have to do so. While the literature circles usually related to the class focus, independent reading remained a time when students had a broad choice of reading materials. Occasionally, writing time involved the class focus, but most of the time students chose their own topics and uses of writing.

Initially we saw independent reading and writing work time as the times of the day when students could focus on language itself by engaging in the process and using those engagements to learn about language and how it functions. When we looked closely at what students were reading and writing, however, we realized that they were pursuing their own personal questions through what they chose to read and write. Some were working through family or peer issues, while others were pursuing information on favorite artists, snakes, or dinosaurs. By maintaining the open-ended nature of work time, we could support children's explorations of their own "kid" topics. A whole-class study on each of these topics is not possible, but children still need the opportunity to pursue personal interests in the classroom. As teachers, we see our role as both supporting and pushing children as learners. Reading and writing work time support children's interests, while the class focus challenges them to consider new perspectives.

Another structure that can support children's explorations of individual topics is expert projects where students investigate any topic of personal interest. In this case, there is no class focus. We used to believe that teachers should schedule expert projects once or twice a year so that students would be able to pursue diverse topics. The problem was that these expert projects often seemed too much like our old units—students chose a topic and collected facts and information without any real sense of broader issues or questions to drive their inquiry. Now, instead of assuming that expert projects have to be scheduled at a particular time, we listen to our students. Sometimes, as they share and present their inquiries, it becomes obvious that their new questions are extremely diverse, and it is important for children to pursue individual questions. At that point, we encourage them to move into small-group and individual inquiries, rather than moving into a new class focus.

In this book, we focus on children's inquiries within a class focus because that's where we began our work with inquiry and have the most experience. For those who want to explore classroom structures where children engage in individual or small-group projects that are not tied to a class focus, we suggest reading about the Explorers' Club (Copenhaver 1992) and expert projects (Copeland 1994).

The Inquiry Cycle as a Curricular Frame

As we explored how to move from our beliefs about inquiry into an inquiry-based curriculum, we found ourselves increasingly turning to the authoring cycle (Harste, Short, and Burke 1988) as a curricular framework. We had all worked with the cycle in thinking about reading and writing in our classrooms and found that it supported our decision-making about curriculum. The cycle served as a bridge that connected our beliefs to specific classroom activities by providing an organizational framework within which we could select engagements and make decisions with our students. Our old frameworks had been sequential scope-and-sequence charts that were based on behaviorist, hierarchical models of learning. Carolyn Burke helped us see that the authoring cycle was not just about reading and writing, but about learning itself. Through this cycle, we came to see authoring as a metaphor for learning and inquiry.

Figure 1.3 presents the authoring cycle as a curricular framework for inquiry (Short and Harste, with Burke 1996). (We will return to this cycle in greater depth in Chapter 8.) The arrows in the cycle go both ways, indicating that there is continual movement back and forth between the different aspects of the inquiry process, rather than a specific sequence or hierarchical order.

The cycle begins with building from students' own life experiences so that they can draw perspectives and connections from those experiences to inform their inquiry. From these personal connections, students move into broad explorations of the topic or focus. These explorations give them time for observations and conversations as they "wander and wonder" through exploration centers and browse a wide range of materials and objects. Through these explorations, they build new understandings about the topic and gradually search out the questions that they want to pursue through further inquiry. Once students have selected a question to pursue in greater depth, they examine that question through different perspectives by thinking collaboratively with other learners, investigating their question through multiple knowledge systems, and using a wide range of sign systems to construct meanings.

Through their research, they encounter many new ideas that create confusions and contradictions. They need time to attend to those differences and to reflect on what those ideas mean to them. At some point, they pull together their investigations to share informally or to present formally to other learners. These presentations give learners an opportunity to determine what it is they know and where they still have questions. After presenting their ideas to others, students need time to plan new inquiries by reflecting on what they have learned and their

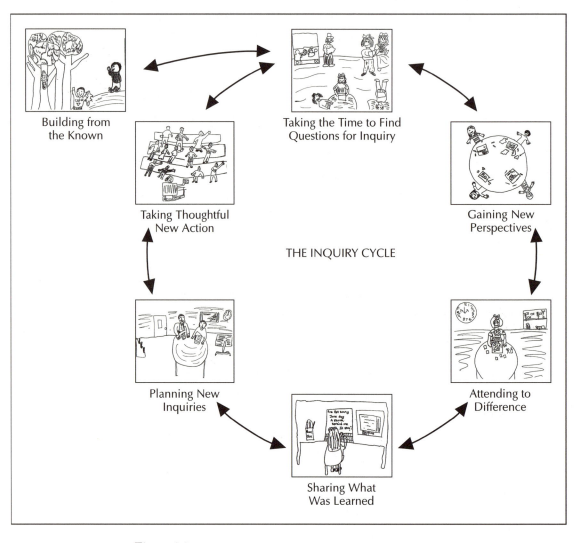

Building from
the Known

Taking the Time to Find
Questions for Inquiry

Taking Thoughtful
New Action

Gaining New
Perspectives

THE INQUIRY CYCLE

Planning New
Inquiries

Attending to
Difference

Sharing What
Was Learned

Figure 1.3
The Authoring Cycle as a Curricular Framework for Inquiry

process of learning, and thinking about the actions they now want to take as learners. These actions include thinking about where they want to move next as inquirers and how they will use what they have learned from this inquiry to change how they think and act in their world. Because the cycle is recursive, students do not move step by step through the cycle, but continually move back and forth depending on their needs as learners.

While this cycle provided a framework that enabled us to think about organizational structures to support students within a particular class focus or individual inquiry, we still had many questions about connecting the different inquiries over time. Each focused study seemed to be a separate entity and, while the inquiry within a particular focused study was powerful, students did not necessarily make connections across the different studies, nor did the studies flow into one another. We wanted to establish an environment where students expected connection, but without forcing or restricting those connections, so we began to explore broad concepts as a curricular structure.

Connecting Curriculum Through a Broad Concept

We wanted to move into an inquiry approach where students pursued topics and questions of significance to them and where one inquiry flowed into the next in an endless cycle or spiral of learning. However, we didn't want to ask students to list what they wanted to study without a supportive context in which they were encouraged also to consider new potentials. In addition, we knew that we needed to think about possibilities for the coming school year without predetermining the curriculum. The more we worked with a broad concept, the more we came to believe that it offered a structure that supported, not restricted, an inquiry-based curriculum.

For us, a broad concept serves as an umbrella that students and teachers can use to encompass a wide range of topics, themes, and ideas. It does not limit the possibilities for class and student inquiries, but provides a point of connection. When we used topics such as community helpers or the Civil War to integrate the curriculum, the connections between subject areas often seemed trite or forced. In contrast, broad concepts, such as Cycles, Change, Systems, Sense of Place, Interdependence, and Discovery, provide many possible points of connection that naturally weave across the day and year and do not limit the topics and questions that students can pursue.

Using the Broad Concept to Support Our Planning to Plan

One of the first ways we found the broad concept useful was in our own planning as teachers before the school year began. Dorothy Watson (Watson, Burke, and Harste 1989) makes the point that as teachers we engage in "planning to plan," but the actual plan is what we create with children. Our question was how to engage in planning to plan in a way that would not predetermine the topics and themes for the school year, but would still give us a framework within which we could think about possibilities and consider topics and resources. The broad concept provided us with a focus around which we could brainstorm a web of possible areas of study. We knew the actual plan would be created with the children, but working with the broad concept gave us a way to think about the curriculum and the classroom learning environment for the coming school year.

Beginning the School Year Through the Broad Concept

The broad concept was a useful place to start the school year. We did not want to ask students during the first week of school to list what they wanted to study. We knew from past experience that this kind of brainstorming leads to lists of general interests and school topics, rather than meaningful issues and questions that have the potential to push students' understandings. Students need time to become a community (Peterson 1992) and to establish a supportive context within which they can consider possible topics and areas of study. By starting the year with the broad concept, we were not determining the topics of study, but we did provide a focus from which the class could begin exploring together. It also gave us time to observe and listen to students so that the curriculum could build from their interests and experiences.

Weaving the Broad Concept Across the Year

While we expected the broad concept to support our planning to plan and initial class experiences, we did not expect the broad concept to play an important role in providing curricular and conceptual connections across the school year for both us and our students. As previously mentioned, we had found our earlier thematic units unrelated to each other, our attempts at connection too often forced. It felt as if we would conclude one unit by neatly closing it up in a box and placing it into storage and then getting down a new box and opening it for the next unit. Each unit was separate from the next; students did not realize they could connect understandings from different topics of study.

The broad concept provided a much more natural connection across different class topics and individual student inquiries throughout the school year. This type of broad connection across experiences seemed to us to reflect the complexities of the world but still provide a focus for students and curriculum. In our daily lives outside of school, everything isn't organized around a topic like "Japan" or "bears," but we do continuously make broad connections between experiences to understand them.

The broad concept created a touchstone for curriculum so that students could make connections across their different questions and interests. As Margaret's students explored their family histories, biome studies, life cycle studies of plants and insects, and historical changes in a community, they continuously returned to how each of these reflected the broad concept of Change over Time and so were able to connect history, science, and their own personal lives.

The broad concept also became a way to bring in mandated curriculum topics and still have those topics connect to other areas of study and inquiry. Kathleen was able to connect the mandated fourth-grade study of state history to students' interests in culture and ethnicity. At the beginning of the year, she did not know exactly when the state study would occur, but she knew that she needed to connect it into students' inquiries at some point. As students finished a set of inquiries on culture and ethnicity, she introduced the state study by bringing in resources related to the many different ethnic groups who live in the state of Arizona.

We found that the broad-concept framework supported students as they thought through and used the facts they were gathering as part of their inquiries. Instead of just collecting isolated facts, they used these facts to examine other conceptual issues. For example, in previous thematic units on space, our students had gathered facts on the sizes of and distances between planets. When Jean's students decided to explore space, they were interested in broader issues of how discoveries are made in space and what would happen if we ever discovered another planet with living beings. Students did gather facts, but they did so because they needed them to think about broader issues.

While thematic units purportedly cut across content areas, the division of the curriculum into separate subject areas is still central to the curriculum. An "integrated" unit is based on the idea that the subject areas are at the center of the curriculum, but they just need to be integrated more. The thematic unit is used as a vehicle to cover the traditional subject areas and to engage children in reading and writing. Through the broad concept, we were able to move to a primary focus on inquiry, where students used knowledge systems and sign systems as tools to pursue their inquiries.

While we all started out at the same point in our classrooms by exploring Discovery as a broad concept and we shared some ideas about inquiry as an approach to curriculum, the actual inquiries that took place in each of our classrooms were quite divergent. These differences indicated to us that the structures and frameworks we were creating in our classrooms supported negotiation with our students and weren't simply another way to impose our agenda onto them. Inquiry was not a new set of procedures or lesson plans that we could pass on to each other, but a way of thinking about curriculum with our students in a way that enabled them to find and examine questions significant in their lives.

Conclusion

In the rest of this book, we tell stories of what occurred in our classrooms and in our work with each other as we tried to put our beliefs about inquiry into action. As is always the case, there were gaps between what we believed and what we could put into action in our classrooms. In Chapter 2, we describe the history of our teacher research group and how we decided on the notion of Discovery as a broad concept for inquiry.

Chapters 3 through 7 tell the stories of particular classrooms. Each chapter begins with a description of how the broad concept of Discovery was established at the beginning of the year and a brief history of how the year unfolded in terms of the different focus studies that children pursued. Each chapter also includes a description of one or two focus studies to give readers a more in-depth look at the ways in which teachers and students worked at inquiry in that classroom. This structure across the chapters demonstrates how we each began at a common point, but then moved in different directions. Our struggles with the roles of teachers and students within a collaborative curriculum are evident throughout these chapters.

As we worked at inquiry in our classroom settings, the inquiry cycle (Short and Harste, with Burke 1996) became an increasingly important organizational framework for how we thought about and planned curriculum. Chapter 8 focuses on the different components of the inquiry cycle through a brief conceptual discussion of each part of the cycle, supported by many examples of engagements and strategies from our classrooms.

The book ends with our reflections on what we have learned from these experiences and the ways in which we have continued to explore inquiry in our classrooms. We think differently now about our classrooms and how to plan curriculum with our students. We continue to work at what it means to have an inquiry-based classroom, and in the final chapter we describe some of our current efforts as well as our lingering questions.

2 Are We There Yet? Beginning Our Voyage of Discovery and Inquiry

THE BELIEFS about inquiry we shared in Chapter 1 grew out of many discussions with each other as well as experiences in our own classroom settings. However, our original reason for working together was not to explore inquiry, but to examine questions about children's understandings of history and culture. Our interest in these questions grew out of a graduate course where we engaged in inquiries around the broad concept of Discovery. This experience led us to design a teacher research study to examine children's understandings in greater depth. Our research included not only planning for how we would conduct research in our own settings, but also thinking through ways to organize curriculum in our classrooms. We found ourselves increasingly concerned with developing classroom learning environments and curricula that would support students as they explored history and culture. Our attention turned to inquiry and how to construct an inquiry-based curriculum with our students. We also came to increasingly value the role that the group was playing in our curriculum planning.

While we knew that the actual curriculum plan would be created with our students, we engaged in "planning to plan" (Watson, Burke, and Harste 1989) to think through possibilities. One of the questions we frequently receive from other teachers is how to plan when so much of the curriculum is negotiated with children. We spent a great deal of time carefully thinking through possibilities and pulling together materials and resources before the school year began. We found that in many ways we had to be more prepared than before because we needed to respond flexibly and quickly to children's interests and questions. While thinking through inquiry involved a different thinking process for us as teachers than when we planned thematic units, we did not just sit back and wait to see what would happen. We discussed and thought through many possibilities. This chapter describes our thinking and our planning-to-plan documents.

Living the Process of Inquiry as Teachers

Because inquiry was a term that was appearing frequently in conversations at conferences and many local teachers were asking questions about using literature within science and social studies, Kathy decided to offer an intensive summer course called "Integrating Literature into Inquiry." A number of the teachers in this course knew each other from previous courses and projects and so had already learned to think and work together.

Kathy used the inquiry cycle (Short and Harste, with Burke 1996) as a curricular framework to organize the course so that teachers could find and pursue their own questions about curriculum. She believed that before teachers considered issues of curriculum, however, they needed to experience an inquiry cycle for themselves. Because the Columbus Quincentenary was occurring the following year and was raising contention and debate among local teachers and in the national media, she began the course with a short inquiry cycle around the broad concept of Discovery and a more specific focus study on Columbus. From this shared experience, teachers then moved into their own areas of interest related to inquiry, curriculum, and literature.

The inquiry cycle around Discovery began with engagements where teachers could explore their own understandings about discovery through reading, conversation, and experience centers. They also read several children's books about Columbus (Fritz 1980; Meltzer 1990) along with journal articles and editorials that reflected many different points of view about the Columbus event. Class and small-group discussions were often quite intense as teachers considered new perspectives. Some felt a sense of betrayal that what they had been taught as children and what they had taught as teachers was biased exclusively to a European perspective and based on myths and misinformation. They began to ask questions about other ways in which history in schools reflected only one group's perspective. Their interests and questions resulted in a class collection of books, magazines, articles, and editorials related to Columbus and other events in American history.

From these experiences, small groups made webs of possible topics, issues, and questions they might pursue related to the broad concept of Discovery and the more specific focus on the Columbus event. These were shared to create a whole-class web of possible topics for small-group inquiries. Teachers then signed up for the topic or issue they wanted to pursue.

The focused study on the Columbus event was an important shared experience for the class. Kathy established initial structures to support the class, but these structures were then negotiated and adjusted as teachers actually began working in the small groups. Within their groups, they could talk openly about their own personal connections to the readings and issues and make choices of topics they wanted to pursue. While some groups chose more traditional content topics, such as the ocean, navigation, mapmaking, or the Renaissance, others engaged in a critical examination of issues of history and culture, such as Native American world views, "advanced" and "primitive" cultures, and a critique of books for children about Columbus.

Teachers spent several days working in their small groups and gathering books, materials, and artifacts. They browsed through these sets, taking research notes on what they were finding out about the topic and the questions that they had. They also chose a smaller, more focused text set from their collection for a literature circle discussion. Their research notes from these experiences were used to create a small-group web of issues and themes on their topic and to list related materials and engagements. These webs were shared with the rest of the class through handouts and displays.

Teachers' reflections on this focused study indicated that it had changed many of their perspectives about the Columbus event and the ways in which they would share this event with their students. For many, it also raised broader issues about history and culture and made them aware of the need to pursue a range of perspectives on any historical event and to search for primary sources, not just depend on others' interpretations. They thought about the actions they could take in their own teaching contexts and later presented their small-group Columbus inquiries to teachers at a large local conference.

The Columbus focused study moved the class through an inquiry cycle. This shared context and "lived-through" experience provided powerful points for connection and discussion about inquiry and the use of the inquiry cycle as a curricular framework. The focused study provided a demonstration of a possible structure teachers might use in their inquiry projects for the class. It also provided a context for challenging thematic units and the topics and activities typically used in these units. The Columbus focused study was an invitation for teachers to think in different ways about their classrooms. They could accept or reject this invitation as they made decisions about their individual projects for the course.

During the rest of the course, teachers read and discussed professional readings about inquiry, Kathy made presentations about inquiry and curriculum, small groups met to work and think together on professional issues, and individuals read children's books as well as professional materials in the class library. Because it was summer and teachers could not work with their students, most used their inquiry projects as a time to engage in planning to plan, relating it to a class theme or topic. These inquiries were quite diverse and included such activities as looking at plants and trees through artistic, literary, and scientific perspectives and using a broad concept (Interdependence, Perspectives, Conflict, Adaptation, Culture, Community, or Mysteries) to organize the school year.

Several teachers focused on their own learning instead of working on classroom plans. They chose something new they wanted to learn about and kept a journal of their learning process. One person looked at what she could do personally about pollution in her home and personal life; another took a class on papermaking. Others researched and collected children's books and activities related to topics such as geography, the ocean, coyotes, Japan, and informational books for young children. The projects were shared at a celebration on the last day of class through interactive displays and handouts for class members.

As the course came to an end, participants were both excited and tense as they contemplated new actions and perspectives as well as new questions. Some of these questions related to earlier class discussions about the issue of protection versus perspective. These discussions had begun with the notion that both teachers and authors of children's biographies and historical fiction seem to feel they need to protect children from the harsh realities of life. In so doing, however, they provide children with misconceptions and misinformation. The class talked about the importance of helping children gain a perspective on historical events, rather than trying to protect them. At the same time, the teachers wondered about how much young children really need to know. Was it important for them to know that Columbus chopped off the hands of American Indians who did not bring him gold? Couldn't they provide children with more realistic and diverse perspectives without getting into all of the details? These questions led many teachers to ask questions about other historical events and to read alternative versions of American history and rethink how they were presenting history. Other questions related to issues that several readings had raised about the limitations of young children's understandings about history and culture (Levstik 1987).

Many left the course feeling unsettled, some because "facts" about American History that they had accepted all of their lives had suddenly been questioned, others because they had a sense that they could be using something different in terms of curriculum but weren't quite sure what that something was. Some teachers made adjustments in how they taught thematic units; others began to rethink their whole approach through an inquiry perspective. Many were intrigued by the concept of inquiry and knew it had potential but felt the need for firsthand experience in working at inquiry with students. Would inquiry make a difference in the classroom? Was inquiry just a slightly different twist on thematic units? Did inquiry really represent a different way of thinking and planning in the classroom?

The summer seminar left us with many questions about inquiry and children's understandings, but we did not initially intend to pursue them as a group. We returned to teaching, working at inquiry-based curriculum in our individual settings. The following spring, however, we were involved in a university seminar on research in children's literature. As we explored this research, we became increasingly concerned that young children's understandings were often studied in contexts that did not support them in building a sense of history or in considering the perspectives of others around them. Our work with young children had convinced us that they were capable of understanding much more than researchers had found in their studies.

While some researchers claim that young children have difficulty in dealing with history and diverse perspectives (Levstik 1987), we believe that they have underestimated children's abilities to understand. The work of Piaget (1977) has been used to argue that the discipline of history is a formal operation developed in late adolescence and that young children are egocentric and do not recognize that others may have different perspectives. Much of the research on young children has occurred in clinical settings or through short-term classroom experiences that have not provided children with a strong context from which to make sense of history and culture. We argued that if educators wanted to examine children's understandings, they needed to first create classroom environments that would support children's thinking and then study these understandings over longer periods of time.

We believe that children's difficulties with the concepts of history and culture are the result of experience rather than developmental or cognitive stages. The difference between adults and children is in the amount and kinds of experiences they have had with the world, rather than qualitative differences in their cognitive abilities and structures (Harste, Woodward, and Burke 1984). Young children are not unable to understand history and culture; they simply do not yet have the wealth of experiences and knowledge of older children and adults. Based on these beliefs, we began working on curriculum that we felt would build a rich context within which we could explore their understandings.

Because Kathleen, Margaret, Gloria, Julie, and Jean were all teaching first or second grade at the time, we saw the opportunity to examine young children's understandings in our own classroom contexts. Our schools were in different parts of the city and served quite different student populations, so we felt that working together would give us broader and deeper insights into children's understandings. Kathy sent a research proposal to the University of Arizona's Columbus Quincentenary Program to fund materials we would need for our research, such as books, audiotapes, and microphones. When the grant was funded, we began meeting and thinking together.

Working Together as a Teacher Research Group

Our teacher research group met throughout the spring and summer to talk about establishing inquiry-based curricula to support children's explorations of historical and cultural perspectives. We felt that we needed a broad focus for the curriculum, so we looked again at Columbus and the issues that surrounded him. It seemed to us that one of the biggest myths related to Columbus was that he discovered America. Our negative feelings about Columbus's supposed discovery was balanced by the excitement we felt about the idea of discovery within inquiry, so we decided to use Discovery as a broad concept that would weave across the curriculum throughout the year.

For many of us, this was the first time we had used a broad concept within an inquiry cycle framework. Having a group with whom we could think collaboratively was essential in supporting each of us as we worked through this transition in our teaching. Our teacher research group met every other week in the spring and several times in the summer to think together about possibilities for the next school year. We continued to meet every other week once school began in the middle of August.

Before we initiated the actual study in the fall, most of us changed grade levels. Julie began teaching kindergarten, Margaret stayed in first grade, Jean extended her first- and second-grade multi-age classroom to include third grade, Kathleen moved to fourth grade, Gloria moved to fifth grade, and Kathy continued teaching graduate students. We soon realized that this range of grade levels was not a problem but an opportunity to look at our questions across the elementary grades and with diverse student populations. Our students came from a range of cultural backgrounds, but were primarily Mexican American and European American with some Yacqui, Hopi, Tohono O'odham, African American, and Asian American children.

In our meetings during the school year, we discussed the types of data we were collecting. We developed a fall and spring interview through which we could examine children's historical and multicultural understandings. We taped and transcribed literature discussions in each classroom throughout the year and collected related student artifacts, such as webs and journals.

During our meetings we shared our field notes and teacher journals to help us evaluate and plan the classroom learning experiences. At the end of the year, we used these notes, journals, and artifacts to write histories of our individual classrooms for that school year. Writing these histories enabled us each to capture as many of the year's events as possible. These histories have been a major source of our later writing about these experiences.

We continued meeting the following year to analyze the talk in the transcribed literature discussions. Through this analysis, we developed a taxonomy of categories to describe children's understandings of history and culture. In addition, we did an initial analysis to compare children's responses on the fall and spring interviews.

We shared our research with different audiences through formal and informal presentations and several publications (Crawford et al. 1994; Laird et al. 1994; Short et al. 1992). Having the opportunity to discuss our research with others helped us stretch our thinking and look critically at what occurred in our classrooms. Several group members analyzed data for university classes and other presentations and then brought questions and comments from these presentations back to the group for consideration. These many opportunities to share and process our thinking with each other and with other educators allowed us to return to our data and classrooms with new perspectives.

While many of us had previously participated in various study groups and in teacher research, we had not worked closely with other teachers in thinking through and reflecting on the daily life of the classroom. Our group became a place where we could collaboratively think through possibilities for curriculum. Our planning-to-plan sessions then became the basis for actually planning curriculum with our students.

Thinking Together About Curriculum Possibilities

In our planning-to-plan meetings during the spring and summer, we talked about a wide range of curriculum possibilities for the coming school year. We began by webbing our understandings of Discovery and listing possible themes and topics. We gathered pieces of children's literature on Columbus to support our brainstorming about issues and concepts that might develop from the Columbus event. We also read professional articles and chapters about the controversies on Columbus and book reviews on Columbus materials (Bigelow 1992; Rethinking Schools 1991). As we read, we shared and added to our web.

Once we had developed our web of possibilities, we began putting together lists of text sets for each of the areas on the web. Text sets (Short 1992) are groups of conceptually related picture books that children read and discuss in small groups. Generally each set contains five to fifteen books (fiction, nonfiction, and poetry) that present a variety of perspectives on the same topic. Children read different books from the set and then come together to share what they have read and compare the books by searching for similarities and differences among them. We felt that text sets would be particularly appropriate for these inquiries because the books and materials in the sets could be selected to reflect different cultural perspectives and contemporary as well as historical time periods. In each set, we listed some books that reflected ethnocentric European perspectives on Columbus so that children would become aware of and could critique that viewpoint (see Figure 2.1).

Changing Misperceptions and Stereotypes
The People Shall Continue
Gila Monsters Meet You at the Airport
Crow Boy
The True Story of the Three Little Pigs
Everyone Knows What a Dragon Looks Like
The Adventures of Connie and Diego
People
William's Doll
Kevin's Grandmother

Cultural Encounters
Corn Is Maize
Encounter
Sky Dogs
All Pigs on Deck
El Chino
Pueblo Boy
Mrs. Katz and Tush
Angel Child, Dragon Child

Discovery
The Very First Last Time
How Many Days to America?
Island of the Skog
Company's Coming
Seven Blind Mice
Who Shrank My Grandmother's House?
The Wise Woman and Her Secret
The Discovery of the Americas
The Flame of Peace: A Tale of the Aztecs

Family Stories (Change over Time)
Family Pictures
Aunt Flossie's Hats
Roxaboxen
The Keeping Quilt
From Me to You
Birthday Presents
Grandma's Bill
This Quiet Lady
Something from Nothing

Perspectives on the Columbus Voyages
The People Shall Continue
Encounter
Follow the Dream
The Discovery of the Americas
The Tainos
Columbus Day
The Boy Who Sailed with Columbus
Before Columbus
Discovering Christopher Columbus
Morning Girl

DISCOVERY

Ownership
Jamaica's Find
Brother Eagle, Sister Sky
Jack and the Beanstalk
The Auction
My Place
Nettie's Trip South
Summer Wheels
I Was Walking Down the Road
Christopher Columbus

Living in Harmony with Nature and Other Peoples
Red Ribbons for Emma
Tonibah and the Rainbow
And Still the Turtle Watched
The People Who Hugged Trees
Peace Begins with You
A River Ran Wild
The Land of Gray Wolf
Where the Forest Meets the Sea
Keepers of the Earth

Greed
Dragonfly's Tale
The Magic Fish
Rumpelstiltskin
Borreguita and the Coyote
King Midas
Iktomi and the Boulder
Coyote &

Scientific Investigation and Exploration
To Space and Back
The Day We Walked on the Moon
Eyewitness: Explorer
How Did We Find Out About Germs
Outward Dreams
Galileo and the Universe
A Weed Is a Flower
Explorers and Mapmakers

Navigation and Mapmaking
The Glorious Flight
Follow the Drinking Gourd
The Seeing Stick
Three Days on a River in a Red Canoe
Rosie's Walk
As the Crow Flies
Seeing Earth from Space
Prince Henry the Navigator
Maps: From Here to There
Christopher Columbus: How He Did It

Figure 2.1
Teacher Brainstorming Web of Text Sets on Discovery (Steffey and Hood 1994)

We also brainstormed possible activities and engagements. As we thought about initial engagements that might create a context for exploring Discovery, we realized that we needed a way to examine children's current understandings. We developed a small-group and whole-class interview, which we tried out in our classrooms during that spring and revised as a result of that trial. We also taped and analyzed students' discussions of several text sets in literature circles. By working through some of our data collection strategies with students in the spring, we were able to more effectively plan to plan over the summer.

We continued to develop the text sets and the interview throughout the summer. As we thought about possible engagements for the fall, we knew we would need to spend time at the beginning of the year developing the concept of Discovery, tapping into children's current understandings and experiences, and creating a sense of community. We brainstormed lists of possible initial engagements that focused on children's own lives and cultures. These engagements could begin with a focus on self-discovery and classroom community, which we thought might lead to a focus on children's families and communities and then to changes over time and changes over cultures. These explorations could help children move from concepts close to their lives to cultures and time periods that are more distant. We hoped they would understand that different cultures view the same events from different perspectives and that people of other time periods lived their lives in different ways. However, we were well aware that once we began actually planning with the children, they might go in entirely different directions and that these engagements and text sets might not be used at all, or might become support materials for a different inquiry focus.

Because the Columbus Quincentenary was occurring that fall, we knew there would be a great deal of discussion in the media and local communities about the Columbus event. We assumed that at some point this media coverage and our initial explorations of self, community, and change would lead to a more intensive consideration of resources and materials about Columbus. Children could then generate issues and questions related to the Columbus events, the discoveries of the Americas, and the quincentenary as well as our broader focus on Discovery. Whole-class and small-group inquiries could be established around these questions so that children would have time to explore several issues in depth and to share their research with classmates. While we were uncertain about the specific focus of the groups, we put some tentative text sets together that could be used by these groups. Because we did not know where children would go with their inquiries, we were unsure about the nature of the concluding events beyond the children's presenting their small-group inquiries to each other. We did list some possibilities, although ultimately these were never used.

Based on our brainstorming, we created a planning-to-plan document, which contained our interview and listed possible engagements. This document became a resource for each of us, particularly at the beginning of the year. (We have included a copy of this document at the end of this chapter.) It is important to remember that the brainstorming and careful preparation we engaged in as a group was a significant resource for each of us, but was *not* imposed onto the children. Each classroom built from our planning-to-plan ideas, but once children became part of the process of planning, the actual curriculum changed dramatically.

Beginning the School Year

While the curriculum in each classroom went in different directions because of students' interests, we all began the year similarly. We interviewed our students and planned engagements that would encourage students to explore and develop their own understandings of the broad concept of Discovery. Because we believed that the initial engagements needed to be built from children's own life experiences, we used similar engagements at the beginning of the year to encourage children to bring their personal experiences and connections into the classroom. From these initial engagements, each classroom curriculum then developed in very different directions.

Examining Children's Understandings

As part of planning to plan, we created an interview that we agreed to conduct in our classrooms during the first several weeks of school. The interview would serve as a research tool and to inform our teaching. As teachers, we often make assumptions about what children know rather than involve them in experiences that will allow us—and them—to explore their current understandings. We wanted to begin with engagements that would let us really listen to our students.

In composing the interview, we developed a set of engagements that we felt would allow us to examine children's understandings of history and their ability to consider more than one perspective. In small groups of three or four, children were first asked, "Who are famous people you know?" and "What are things that happened long ago?" We asked students to name people who were famous to them and people anybody would know. (We made this distinction because we found that kindergarten and first-grade children tended to answer the question with only the names of people in their family or school.) The children's responses were written on small slips of paper by the teacher or one of the children. The children then glued these papers onto a long sheet of paper to create a time line that ran from "long ago" to "now." In the same small groups, children brainstormed ideas for two webs. For the first web, they were asked, "What do you know about Columbus?" and for the second, "What do you know about the discovery of America?"

From these webs and time lines, we were able to get a sense of our students' current understandings of history. The kindergarten children, for example, put all of the events and people at the "long ago" end of their time line, lumping events that happened hundreds of years ago with events that happened to them the previous week. Fifth graders confused the Pilgrims with Columbus. Some were aware of the controversy about Columbus but were not sure about the nature of this controversy. Few said anything about Native peoples (see Figure 2.2).

In the second part of the interview, we explored children's ability to understand different perspectives. First, we put the Columbus webs from each of the groups on the wall and asked, "Why do we all have different ideas? Why didn't we all say the same things?" We also used two read-aloud books, followed by class discussions. We first read *Best Friends* (Kellogg 1986), which is about two friends who are having a disagreement. We stopped near the end of the story when one character declares to the other, "It's not fair," and asked, "How do you feel about this problem?

What do you think the problem is?" We were particularly interested in whether the children would consider only the narrator's point of view or whether they would also consider the other child's perspective. The second read-aloud was *A Picture Book of Christopher Columbus* (Adler 1991), which takes Columbus's perspective, although it does mention that Columbus's men were cruel to the Indians. Children were asked, "What do you think of this story?" and "How do you think these particular Native Americans might have felt about Columbus?"

We realized later that this initial interview was limited by our own understanding of history as simply a collection of important events, dates, and people. Our interview did not include history as a perspective and a way of researching (Gagnon 1988). At the end of the year when we

Figure 2.2
Sample of Student
Responses to
Interview Questions

Who is Christopher Columbus?	**What do you know about the discovery of America?**
I think he sells coffee. (age 7)	The Vikings discovered America. (age 10)
He might have been a pirate. (age 9)	Nobody discovered it but the Indians. (age 6)
He lost track of the trail and days later he met up with Nina. (age 10)	Most people died—it was hot and there was no water. (age 6)
First to sail the seven seas. (age 7)	The Indians lived there before Columbus discovered it. (age 9)
Author of "Jack and the Beanstalk." (age 5)	Before human beings lived here, dinosaurs lived here. (age 6)
He had the crew do all his killing and chopping off work. (age 10)	First came the Indians, then came the Mexicans, and then came the White people. (age 7)
He called the people Indians because he thought he was in India. (age 9)	America was found by the Indians and Pilgrims. (age 10)
He discovered Plymouth Rock. (age 8)	America was a state. (age 8)
Never heard of him. (age 5)	Indians used to say the Pledge of Allegiance. (age 5)
I saw him on TV. He's a basketball player. (age 6)	There is fifty states in America. (age 9)
He went on a boat—the *Mayflower.* (age 8)	A girl discovered it. (age 5)
He discovered Tucson. (age 6)	One guy discovered Greenland, Iceland, and America. (age 8)

repeated the interview, we added a small-group discussion of the questions "What is history and the past?", "What do you think people mean when they talk about history and the past?", "Why do we look at history?", and "If you wanted to know about the past, what would you do?"

Children's responses to these interviews gave us a sense of their understanding of discovery, time, history, and perspective as we considered possibilities for initial engagements in our classrooms. In planning to plan, we realized we needed to explore self-discovery and family and community history before moving to more complex historical and cultural concepts. During these initial explorations, we concentrated on exploring students' current experiences and developing concepts related to discovery, time, and perspective.

Exploring Discovery, Time, and Perspective

We used our brainstormed list of possible engagements as a resource in thinking about initial experiences, but the particular experiences in each classroom varied. Our first focus was on self-discovery and classroom community. To encourage children to think about the concept of Discovery, each classroom started a large web on this concept to which ideas and connections could gradually be added. During the first week of school, several teachers asked children to discover something new about the room. Others took their classes on a walk around the school to see if they could discover anything new. Another curricular engagement, "Getting to Know You" (Short and Harste, with Burke 1996) involved children's interviewing a classmate to discover something about that person, then publishing the interviews in class newspapers. After each experience, children were asked, "What does it mean to discover?" and their ideas were added to the web (see Figures 2.3 and 2.4).

We also wanted to introduce the idea of time, so children researched and made time lines of their own lives. With some of the younger children, a questionnaire was sent home and then used in the classroom to make a personal time line for each child. In other classrooms, children interviewed family members to decide on significant events for their time lines. Teachers also shared literature in which children or adults trace their lives, such as *Family Pictures* (Garza 1990), *Arctic Memories* (Ekoomiak 1990), and *Birthday Presents* (Rylant 1987).

Several classrooms created a class journal to keep track of the history of that classroom. Each day an entry was made by the class or an individual child. Some students later compared what was written in the class journal (public knowledge) with a personal journal (private thoughts) to better understand the differences between Columbus's two journals.

We also wanted children to explore the idea that different people have different opinions and ways of looking at the world and that no one way is "right." We saw this understanding as essential to developing multi-cultural orientations to life (Ruiz 1988). One classroom activity involved constructing graphs. Children's opinions on particular topics or favorite activities were polled and put onto a graph to highlight the differences

Figure 2.3
Primary Multi-Age Concept Web on Discovery

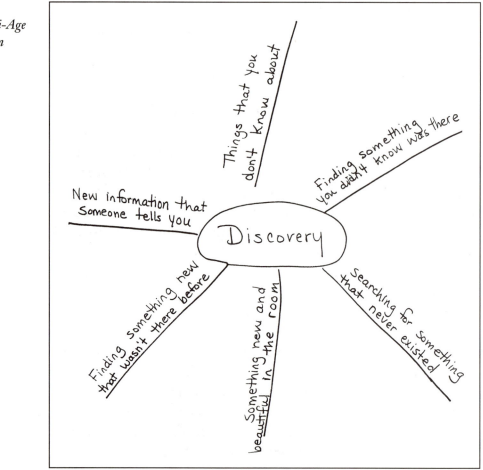

(Whitin, Mills, and O'Keefe 1990). Another form of graph charted children's favorite books and book characters. In addition, particular books were featured in the classroom, such as *Bread Bread Bread* (Morris 1989), which shows families eating different kinds of breads in many different cultural contexts.

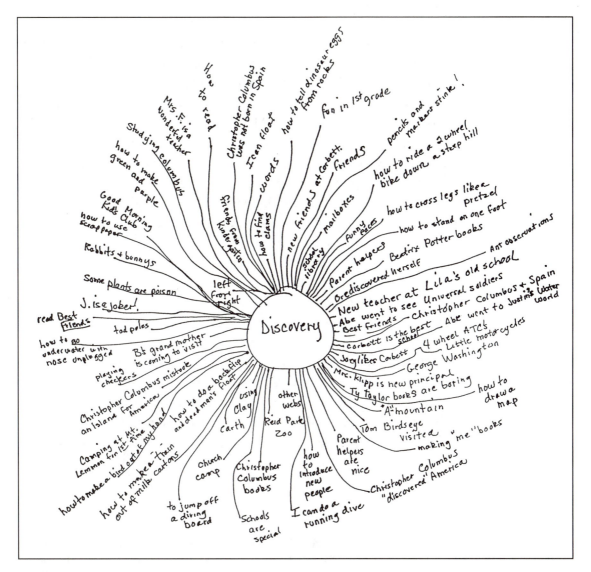

Figure 2.4
First-Grade Concept Web of Personal Connections to Discovery

The focus on children's own lives moved naturally into a focus on their own families and communities. Children's definitions of family ranged from a small family unit to their extended families to their entire cultural group. We created family time lines, collected family stories and told them orally and/or in writing, made graphs of family preferences and activities, and invited family and community members to the classroom to share the history of that community and school.

Children also engaged in whole-class and small-group discussions of picture books that involved older family members telling children the stories of their family. We especially looked for books of families over several generations, such as *Grandma's Bill* (Waddell 1990), *The Keeping Quilt* (Polacco 1988), *Aunt Flossie's Hats* (Howard 1991), *From Me to You* (Rogers 1987), and *Roxaboxen* (McLerran 1991).

These engagements with self, classroom, and family gave children a chance to get to know one another and to explore issues and topics close to their own experiences. Through these engagements, we built a larger conceptual understanding of Discovery, which could then weave across the school year. In each classroom, students developed their own understandings about Discovery that focused their inquiries in different ways (Figure 2.5 shows eleven-year-old Tara's concept web of Discovery).

At the beginning of the year, we were concerned about imposing Discovery onto the children. These concerns eased when we realized that in each classroom the children created their own understandings of Discovery, which led to different conceptual frameworks underlying their work. They determined the actual broad concept that framed their classroom. Julie's and Margaret's students focused on Discovery as change over time, while Jean's students were more interested in history and exploration. Kathleen's, Gloria's, and Kathy's students focused on Discovery as understanding multiple perspectives. Each classroom developed different inquiries that grew out of the school curriculum and their focus as a classroom community.

Conclusion

When we began school in the middle of August, we assumed the Discovery focus would be finished by winter break. In actuality, the focus ended only because the school year ended in May. Each inquiry study led naturally into new topics and questions in a continuous cycle that was unique to each group of students and each classroom. We began with similar engagements, but the negotiation of curriculum with our students took each classroom into different inquiries and focused studies.

The unique cycle of inquiry around Discovery that occurred in each classroom is the focus of the next five chapters. In these first two

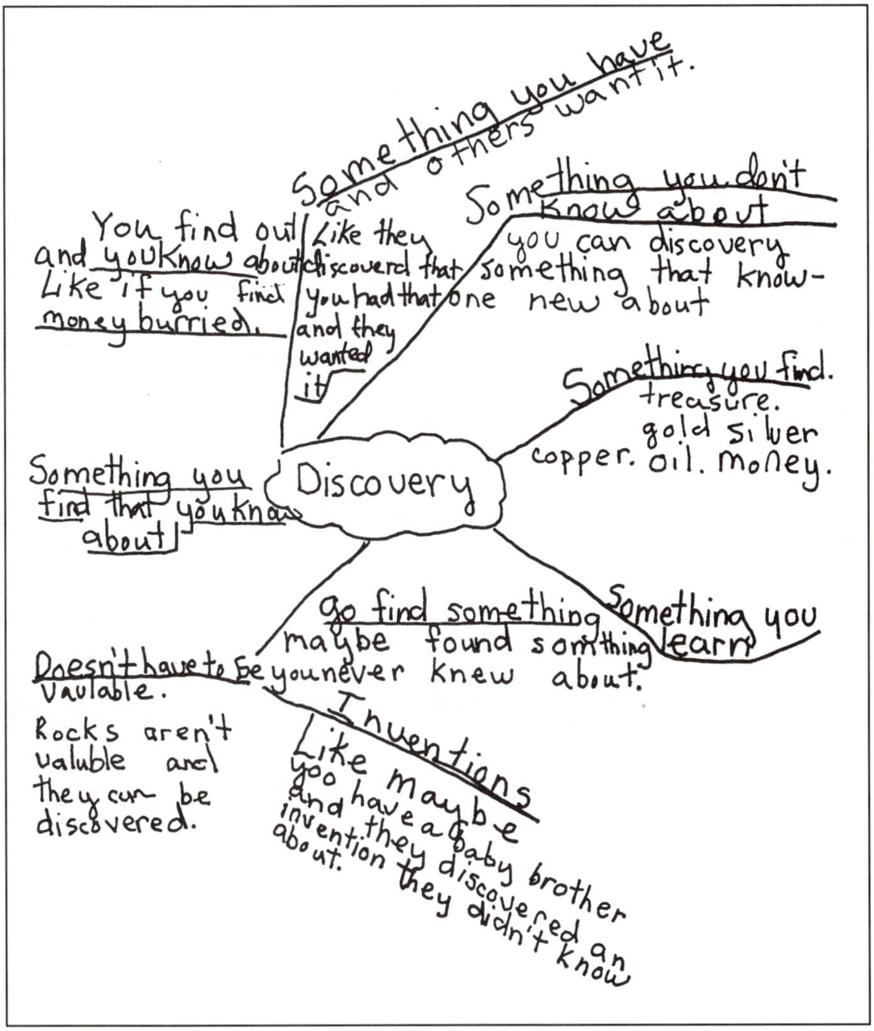

Figure 2.5
Individual Concept Web of Discovery (Tara, Age 11)

chapters, we have highlighted the structures and issues that cut across all of our classrooms. The next five chapters demonstrate how each classroom developed its own understandings about Discovery and its own ways of moving toward inquiry. As each teacher shares her classroom, she will also highlight problems and issues that arose. Many of these came from limitations in our own thinking and our own understanding of inquiry. Later we reflect on how we have changed our approaches to inquiry and the lingering questions that still remain for each of us.

Initiating Events

The major focus of the initiating events is to introduce the concepts of discovery, time, and diverse perspectives. The use of journals and time lines to record history will also be introduced.

Focus on Self-Discovery and Classroom Community
- Ask the children to discover something new about the room or school. Discuss what they have discovered.
- After this experience, ask them, "What does it mean to discover?" and make a large web of their responses.
- Keep adding to this web after other experiences during the first several weeks of school—for example, after doing "Getting to Know You" and asking them to discover something about a classmate.
- Make personal time lines of each child's life. These could be completed by having parents and children complete a questionnaire at home and then doing the actual time line at school.
- Create some way to keep track of the history of the class through either a class journal or time line of the signficant events (daily or weekly).
- Have children compare what is written in a class journal (public knowledge) to personal journals (private thoughts) as a way to compare the two journals Columbus kept.
- Opinion graphs would work for both developing self-concept and high-lighting differences in perspectives among children. One type of graph would be of children's favorite foods, activities, etc., using books, such as *Bread Bread Bread* (Morris 1989). Could also do opinion graphs on their opinions of read-aloud books, book characters, and class issues. These graphs could be collected in a book so they could continue to be available.

Focus on Family and Community Histories and Stories
- Whole-group or small-group discussions of books about families, especially those that show families changing over several generations, such as *From Me to You* (Rogers 1987), *The Keeping Quilt* (Polacco 1988), *Grandma's Bill* (Waddell 1990), and *Once There Were Giants* (Waddell 1989). These might be used as read-alouds or in discussion groups (shared book sets, text sets, or paired books).

- Create family time lines. Could be done at home with families.
- Collect family stories and tell them orally and/or in writing.
- Opinion graphs of family preferences. (Who decides what to have for supper in your family? Show art prints and have children decide which ones their families would hang in their homes.)
- Invite a grandparent, great-grandparent, longtime neighbor, or school administrator to come to the school to share the history of the community and the school.

Inquiry Experiences

Changes over Time and Changes over Cultures

The major focus as we move from concepts close to the children's lives to other cultures and time periods is on the concepts of changes over time and differing cultural perspectives. We are also beginning the inquiry focus on Columbus and gathering ideas for possible inquiry topics.

- Use the two text sets of Change over Time and Changes over Cultures as the core of this exploration in read-aloud and/or small-group discussions. Change over Time involves books such as *Window* (Baker 1991) and *The House on Maple Street* (Pryor 1992). Changes over Cultures would involve books such as *A Country Far Away* (Gray 1989) and *Bread Bread Bread* (Morris 1989) (books where two or more cultures are compared). Could make "change lines" or flow charts to follow changes across time or cultures.
- Begin the whole-class time line, which takes significant events from the participants, personal and family time lines (birth of children, teacher) as well as the people and events that were frequently named in the children's beginning interviews. This time line might be so large that children could actually walk on it. Might use artifacts and pictures as well as print. Could also add Columbus's voyages.
- Visit the Arizona State Museum or a Native American archaeological site.
- Interview parents on what they know about Columbus.
- Brainstorm what the children know about Columbus.
- Keep track of questions and issues that are emerging and may become inquiries.

- Collect newspaper articles on the quincentenary. Read aloud and browse books on the Columbus event.

Columbus Text Sets and Inquiries

Move into whole-class or small-group explorations of concepts and issues related to Columbus using the text sets. Make final decisions about which text sets will be made as we see what inquiry topics children are most interested in exploring. These discussions will be audiotaped; certain discussions will also be videotaped. Possible text sets, which should include contemporary stories, books about Columbus, and books from different cultures (especially Hispanic and Native American cultures), are the following:

Discovery/invasion	Cultural exchanges
Ownership	Exploration (modern and
Greed	historical, imagining the
Harmony versus power	unknown)
Dealing with stereotypes	Journeys
Perspective/illusion	1492 around the world

Browsing sets on European, Native American, and Hispanic cultures will also be established.

Other related topics could include:

Scientific method/discovery	Oceans
Space, the new frontier	Mapmaking
Insects	Inventions/inventors
Navigation	Explorers
Plants and animals (cultural exchanges)	

Concluding Experiences

To pull together the focus on Columbus and discovery, we might have a 1492 day where the classroom becomes the year 1492 and children take on different roles from a variety of different cultures. This experience would pull together their reading and understanding of different perspectives on this experience.

We also discussed the importance of ending with a contemporary focus: "How can you make a difference today?" This might involve the students' talking about issues they can take a stand on today and situations where they see people who don't understand each other and then brainstorming what they might be able to do. The discussions and brainstorming could provide a focus for the rest of the year in terms of children's taking action in their present-day world.

Return to the web of discovery and create a new web.

Finish with the interview.

Fall and Spring Interview

The interview will be conducted in the fall and the spring, with small groups and the whole class, to evaluate children's understandings about history, Columbus, and diverse perspectives.

In Groups of Three or Four

1. Who are famous people you know (that is, famous to you and people anybody would know)?
2. What are things that happened long ago?

As children respond to these two questions, the teacher puts their responses on small cards or slips of paper. The group will then be asked to put the cards on a time line and glue them down in order from long ago to now.

3. What do you know about Columbus?
4. What do you know about the discovery of America?

These two questions will be put on separate webs for each small group.

Whole Class

5. Compare the webs to begin exploring children's understanding of more than one perspective. (Put up the webs from the small groups and ask the students: Why do we have different ideas? Why didn't we all say the same things?)
6. Read a scenario or book on an incident from everyday life where there is more than one perspective, and have a whole-class discussion.
7. Read a simple Columbus book and have the children discuss it. Then ask them, "How do you think these particular Native Americans might have felt about Columbus?"

Final interviews will follow the same procedure, with children in the same small groups. New webs will be made. One extra step is that the children will be asked to compare their new webs with the ones they made in the fall.

3 Sailing the Seven Seas: Using the Tools of Historians and Researchers

Jean Schroeder

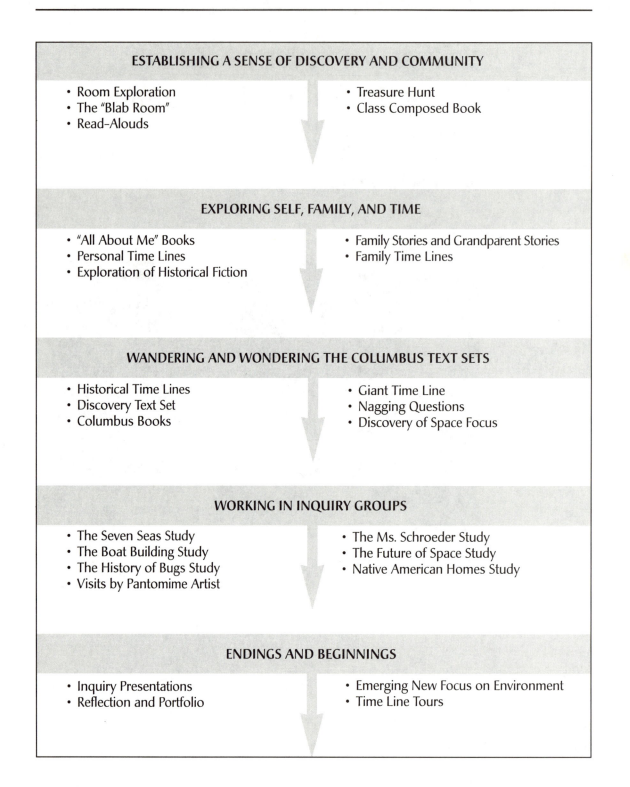

ESTABLISHING A SENSE OF DISCOVERY AND COMMUNITY

- Room Exploration
- The "Blab Room"
- Read-Alouds
- Treasure Hunt
- Class Composed Book

EXPLORING SELF, FAMILY, AND TIME

- "All About Me" Books
- Personal Time Lines
- Exploration of Historical Fiction
- Family Stories and Grandparent Stories
- Family Time Lines

WANDERING AND WONDERING THE COLUMBUS TEXT SETS

- Historical Time Lines
- Discovery Text Set
- Columbus Books
- Giant Time Line
- Nagging Questions
- Discovery of Space Focus

WORKING IN INQUIRY GROUPS

- The Seven Seas Study
- The Boat Building Study
- The History of Bugs Study
- Visits by Pantomime Artist
- The Ms. Schroeder Study
- The Future of Space Study
- Native American Homes Study

ENDINGS AND BEGINNINGS

- Inquiry Presentations
- Reflection and Portfolio
- Emerging New Focus on Environment
- Time Line Tours

I MOVE AROUND my room with the kind of haste that comes with the first-day jitters. The kids are scared and I am too eager. My student teacher and my new teacher aide are wondering what they have gotten themselves into. We are about to embark on a year-long trek back in time, using the tools of historians and researchers as part of our focus on Discovery and children's multicultural and historical understandings.

Although the first day of school is always nerve-racking, the tone that is created that day is crucial to what happens the rest of the year. In addition to the usual first-day nervousness, I was moving from a multi-age class of first and second graders to one that also included third graders. Only three of my twenty-four students were returning. Somehow, we all had to become a family, a community. We needed to quickly establish a sense of belonging and unity that we could build on in order for the year to flow smoothly.

Barry, Peter, and John, my returning students, were influential in setting the stage as their smiles and sense of ease rippled through the class, spreading positive vibes. Their help was invaluable in orienting new class members. They became the experts in the room, explaining policies and procedures, providing answers to questions like "Where's the bathroom?", helping with routines, and locating some of the everyday supplies for learning, such as glue, pencils, paper, and scissors. They helped build the foundation of what became a flourishing community of learners.

The classroom journey portrayed here begins with the class's thinking about Discovery and self, and then moves to their exploring concepts of time and history through time lines. The children's new understandings led them to inquiry questions, which they pursued in small groups. It all culminated in a celebration of learning.

Establishing Community and Exploring Discovery

An accepting and positive environment is a priority for me, so I prepared carefully for the first week, planning engagements that would promote this kind of environment. Composed of collaborative thinkers, the teacher research group became a storehouse of ideas, and I drew upon this resource frequently. In discussions about the broad concept of Discovery, I considered many possible learning experiences for my young students. I began with an exploration of the room. I asked children to check out all the nooks and crannies and to record their discoveries as they went. Returning students were challenged to find new items or changes in the room. After their search, the children gathered at tables and compared notes. When a child saw something no one else had, he or she led the group to the discovery. As the small groups finished talking, the whole class came together and shared their findings. Having thoroughly investigated the room in their exploration, children acquired a sense of ownership and placed a value on talk as a way of learning (Pierce and Gilles 1993).

We also wrote a book the first day—an overwhelming task from a young child's perspective. They discovered that such a task was not only possible, but also enjoyable. Using *Quick as a Cricket* (Wood 1982) as a model, each child completed the pattern "I am as _____ as a _____" to describe and illustrate themselves. The pages were combined into a class book, and the students selected the title *Bright as a Star*. As one of the first read-alouds, the book enabled us to learn about one another and to cohere as a group. *Bright as a Star* quickly became a class favorite. As children revisited it throughout the year, they discovered their own growth, noting what they could do now that they could not do on the first day of school.

The books we read aloud as a class played a vital role in building community, since they became part of our common knowledge and shared experiences. *My Great-Aunt Arizona* (Houston 1992) was particularly important to my class because it addressed multi-age groupings. The students adopted the name "The Blab Room" for our class, a historical detail mentioned in this story in reference to the one-room schoolhouse. They made large portraits of themselves, displayed them in the hall next to our door, and added speech balloons, some of which invited people to come in and ask what a "blab room" was. Enough people accepted this invitation that children found themselves in the role of teachers while adults became the learners. As the year progressed children became aware that everyone in the room was a teacher and a learner and that we were all discovering new ideas.

The children also participated in what I call a "Treasure Hunt." Using a paper listing interests, such as soccer or pets, the students tried to find at least two people in the room who shared these specific interests. They could also add their own ideas to the page. The festive mood during this engagement became a celebration of learning and diversity as children discovered the rich resources within themselves and within their class.

These learning experiences not only highlighted the broad concept of Discovery, but also initiated a camaraderie that carried us through the year. It was from these initial explorations that we began to define Discovery for our class.

Stepping Back in Time

In the context of examining children's multicultural and historical understandings, one of my greatest concerns was developing a concept of the past. The notion of time is very abstract for young children. The teacher research group had talked about using time lines, and this idea appealed to me. I remembered a time line set in the sidewalk at the Arizona Sonoran Desert Museum to demonstrate the period from the origin of the planet Earth to the first appearance of human beings. I liked the idea of "walking" a time line as a way of leading into the past. But where to start? That was easy. Start with the students.

I began reading stories that focused on self and self-concept, such as *I Like Me!* (Carlson 1988). The class decided to make an "All About Me" book. I made a few suggestions for pages, and they chose to include a self-portrait, a family picture, and pages on pets, best friends, feelings, likes and dislikes, and what they would do when they were adults.

By collaborating with their parents to gather information, students were able to make personal time lines. They recorded important events in their lives in research booklets and then chose what they wanted to put on their time lines. As they worked, children talked about what they were including, such as when they had begun to walk or talk. Many of the students seemed to recognize that adults saw these as important milestones. Even children who had not recorded this information in their research booklets tried to incorporate it on their time line (but not always in appropriate time slots!). These discussions helped establish the purpose and use of time lines as students realize that events mark segments of time.

By expanding the focus on self to include the immediate family and then even further to include grandparents, children found themselves strolling into the past in a concrete context. The class collected family stories, stories about themselves or their parents when they were little, and brought them to school, anxious to share them. After reading these stories to the class we typed them, the children illustrated their own stories, and we published them as a class book (Figure 3.1 shows a page from that book).

Through literature discussion children stepped further into the past with grandparent stories. They also talked to their grandparents or older friends and relatives about what it was like when they were little. These

Figure 3.1
Family Story
(Jesus, Age 8)

THE OLD ORANGE TRUCK

I have an orange truck that has been in my family for years. When I grow up, I'll have that truck and when I have kids and they grow up, they'll have that truck.

stories were published as a class newspaper. I invited children to make a family time line at home that included their immediate family and, if possible, their grandparents. These time lines came in all shapes and sizes. Some were family trees. Several went back to the 1800s. One included the terms of office of all the presidents of the United States. Another child's extended back to 1470 on both sides of his family to coincide with our interest in the Columbus quincentenary.

Typically when history is taught in schools, teachers begin at the earliest point in time pertaining to the period of study and move toward the present, asking students to leap into the past rather than building a context to which they can connect their learning. By beginning with the present and themselves and then moving back through time, children were better able to think about and understand the past.

Using Tools to Understand Time and History

I continued to build on the students' obvious enthusiasm for time lines by displaying two commercially produced time lines on Columbus. One was on the 1492 voyage, with each day numbered, and the other was on Columbus himself, with printed captions highlighting significant events in his life. The children were by this time familiar with many texts on Columbus, through read-alouds and book browsing, and had raised questions about the discrepancies among them. Because of the numerous discussions surrounding these issues, they were able to connect the information on the time line with their own understandings about Columbus. Eventually I displayed these two time lines together and immediately we were able to apply the concepts of scale and measurement, because the voyage time line, which covered just seventy-one days, was almost as long as the time line, which covered Columbus's entire life. We added a couple of the children's own time lines, which varied from six to nine years, to help illustrate and clarify the concepts.

During this time we read aloud *The Discovery of the Americas* (Maestro 1991). While there was high interest about when and how people first came to the Americas, there was also much confusion over geographical concepts. A land bridge was something students could not understand until we got out maps and globes and reread the text with these tools at hand. Learning the use of maps and globes became significant as the students moved into inquiry. By demonstrating how these tools could build our understanding of the Maestro book, the children returned to the maps and globes independently to enhance their own research.

All of this time I had been struggling to figure out how to create a time line to actually walk through. My hope was that by bringing a physical sense to time, I could make the concept less abstract. I finally came across some cheap rope that was both light enough to be hung from the ceiling and heavy enough to be easily seen. The rope became a 250-foot time line that ran from 1992 back to 1492. I marked every hundred years with a wide red tape and every ten years with narrow blue tape and hung three markers on the rope: my birth year, the student teacher's birth year, and the teacher aide's birth year. Immediately the kids wanted to know where their birth years would fall.

We then took the time line into the hall and strung it out along the floor to see how far it reached from our classroom. It stretched past the office almost to the library. The children went to the beginning of the time line and walked the 250 feet. Two girls arrived at the far end panting, out of breath, and begging for water!

The class was fascinated by this time line. We hung it from the ceiling in the hall and added each student's birth year by listing the year and everyone in the class who was born that year on a card and taping it to the time line. They wanted to add other markers as well. They decided to adjust the time line to begin with Columbus's birth year in 1451, and made a 1492 card to mark his voyage. In small groups the children brainstormed what they thought were important events that we might include. Most of these turned out to be personal events they had marked on their personal time lines. We had to distinguish between events that are important in a family and those that are important to a larger audience. I pulled the class together for a brief discussion. By using specific examples, the students were able to distinguish between personal and historical events. Each group then made a list of what they wanted to add to the time line. Initially I had intended to supply dates for these markers, but I didn't know when Billy the Kid had died or when baseball was invented. So we went to the library, answered most of our questions, and added the new markers to the time line. The problem of how to mark events that occurred before 1451 was solved by taping a large paper to the wall near the end of the time line and labeling it. All markers for events before 1451 were placed on this paper.

This engagement was the beginning of a class project that lasted until the end of the year. I had ordered a book from one of the Scholastic book clubs called *Do You Know What Day Tomorrow Is?* (Hopkins and Arenstein 1990), in which historical events, inventions, and significant occasions are listed. Organized by the calendar year, this book became part of our morning opening. We read the listings for that day and then voted as a class on which ones to add to the hallway time line. When other possible dates emerged through the course of the day, the class decided whether or not to include them. Slowly we added more and more markers. Students of all ages as well as adults were observed going down the hall with their eyes on the ceiling. (Only once during the school year did I have to do a major repair from students jumping and pulling it down.) Throughout the year many students and teachers asked questions about the time line, so the class decided to give "Time Line Tours." The students webbed out what they thought they needed to tell others about the time line. Using this information, we wrote a brief suggested script, which could be read or ad-libbed. The students formed groups of three, divided the task, found two or three markers on the time line in which they had a particular interest, and practiced. We sent out flyers to all the other classrooms to sign up for Time Line Tours. It was a successful way of sharing our discoveries with the entire school.

For young students, time lines, maps, and globes provided a way to understand the past. Children recognized the usefulness of these tools, and their interest was the incentive for continued exploration. While some children used these tools strictly to order events, others were able to see the effect one event or invention (such as harnessing electricity) had in the course of time. Time lines especially helped students in their research. As they began focusing on interests other than Columbus they found that everything has a history and that history shapes current understanding about many topics.

Identifying Research Questions

Literature and literature circles were at the heart of the students' explorations. As a class we read many of the Columbus books and looked carefully at a text set on Discovery. When the children first began reading I asked them to record any questions they had from their reading on a sheet of paper. These lists of questions were ongoing and kept by the students in a work folder. I asked them to bring their questions to literature circles and suggested they might want to discuss them with the group. (Figure 3.2 shows one student's questions.)

After one of our teacher researcher meetings, when I was feeling confused about where we were heading, I came back to class and decided to

Figure 3.2
*List of Inquiry
Questions
(Miranda, Age 8)*

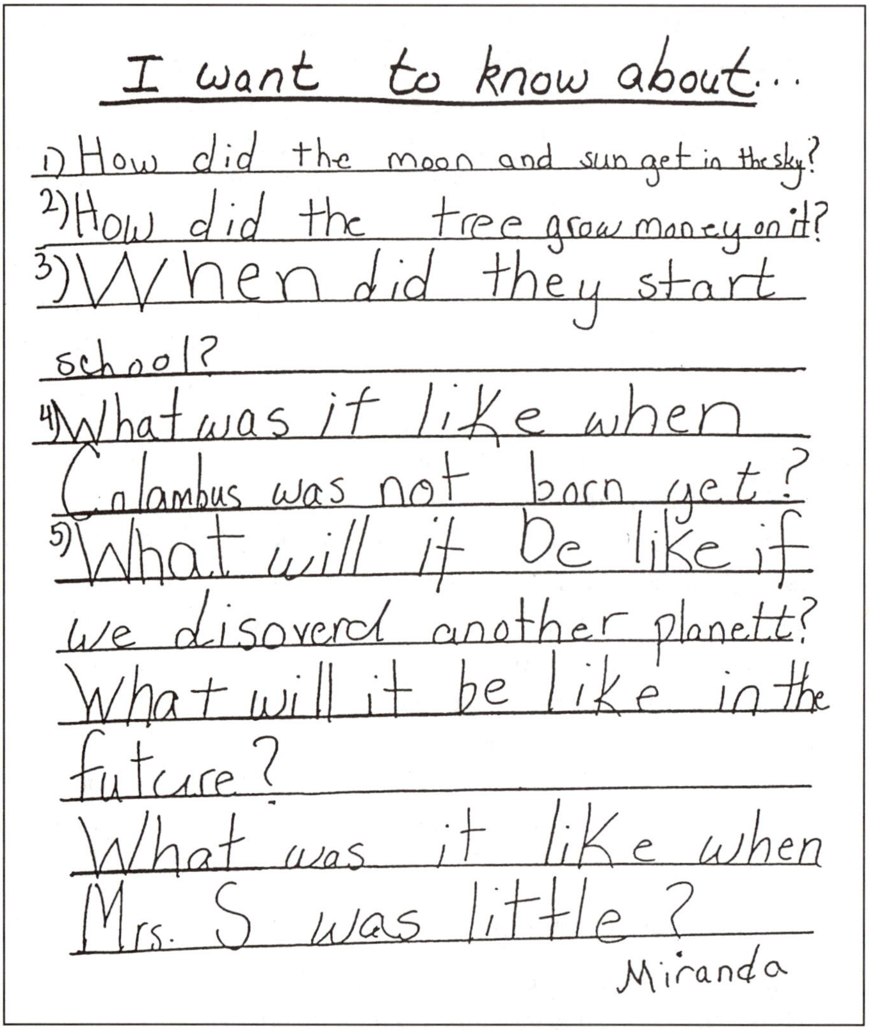

I want to know about...
1) How did the moon and sun get in the sky?
2) How did the tree grow money on it?
3) When did they start school?
4) What was it like when Colambus was not born yet?
5) What will it be like if we disoverd another planett?
What will it be like in the future?
What was it like when Mrs. S was little?

Miranda

focus on the students' questions. We recorded them on butcher paper and then added new ones. Some of their questions were straightforward, such as "How old was Christopher Columbus when he sailed?" and "What is a coastline?" Others had more depth: "Why did they fight?" "Will things be the way the book says?" "How nice were the Native Americans?" This large sheet of questions was posted in the room. As new questions arose they were added and, as others were answered, the answers were recorded and the question checked off. This process highlighted the more thoughtful questions, because the factual questions were quickly answered.

The students then browsed ten text sets looking for one they wanted to read more intensively. Discussion groups formed focusing on such topics as change over time, perspectives, greed, discovery, Columbus, and invasion. The children continued to ask and record questions as they read and discussed. I met several times with each group. My concern about where we were going as a class and how we were going to get there was increasing. I felt the class was scattered and uncollected. The holidays were approaching, and I desperately wanted to pull things together so the move into January would be smooth. The class reviewed the lists of questions in the room. Then, in small groups, they talked about the nagging questions they were still asking, the ones that were really bugging them. Again we met together and recorded the results of their small-group discussions. I was very impressed. Their list of questions covered a wide range—time lines, space, homes of Native Americans, deeper understanding of the 1492 Columbus voyage, lifestyles during the 1400s and 1500s, the history of bugs (when they were first studied and who studied them), what Ms. Schroeder was like when she was little, and the history of medicine. And, of course, the seven seas! What are the seven seas, and did Columbus really sail them? Since early fall this question had kept surfacing, no matter how hard I tried to dismiss it!

I gave the class some time to talk and think. Each child needed to find a question he or she was particularly interested in or some friends they wanted to work with in order to form inquiry groups. Everyone quickly and efficiently situated themselves in a group. Two wanted to study the future of space. Four wanted to know more about the construction of Native American homes of the past. Another four chose to find out how boats are built. A group of three decided to explore the history of bugs. Three others planned on finding out about my sordid past. And the seven seas issue was still swimming around! I finally felt we had a direction in which to move; more important, we were all excited about it.

Moving into Focused Inquiry

To reacquaint the children with the focus of their inquiry after the holiday break, they met in their groups and made lists of what they knew and questions that pertained to their inquiries. The next day we created a web entitled "How to find out . . . " and the children brainstormed ideas, including going to the public library, reading both fiction and nonfiction, checking the atlas and encyclopedia, going to another classroom, networking, visiting the place you are studying, working with someone, taking a field trip, thinking, talking on the phone, and finding an expert. My suggestion of writing letters was met with "I was going to say that" by several children. I gave each group a folder for collecting data, and the class decided on one specific place to keep the folders when they were not in use, to avoid losing them. We were off and running!

To provide a better picture of how these groups functioned, I will follow two of the inquiry groups through the discoveries they made while studying their focus questions. I will describe both the "Seven Seas" group, my least favorite as we started, and the "Ms. Schroeder" group, in which I had a vested interest!

Exploring the Seven Seas

The Seven Seas group began with the questions "What are the seven seas?" and "Did Columbus really sail them?" The class first asked these questions early in the school year, when movies about Columbus were being heavily advertised on television. These questions held little interest for me. I tried hard to ignore them, but they would not go away. When students continued to be interested in them, and a group, consisting of one eight-year-old and three six-year-olds, formed to explore the topic, I looked for ways to support them. To their original two, they added the questions "Who named the seven seas?" "How many seas did Columbus sail to get to China?" and "Does the captain have the boat that Columbus sailed in?"

Over the winter holidays, as I put together beginning text sets for the groups, I found the Seven Seas text set particularly difficult. We had already spent a great deal of time reading and thinking about the Columbus books. Geography books didn't seem to lend themselves to literature discussion, and books on the ocean tended to focus on marine life. I finally decided to put together a set of books on sea voyages, including *How Many Days to America?* (Bunting 1988), *The Voyage of the Ludgate Hill* (Willard 1987), *Sir Francis Drake* (Gerrard 1988), and *The Walloping Window-Blind* (Carryl 1992). I searched in particular for stories and poems that used the expression "sailing the seven seas," but without success. Later I added *Over the Deep Blue Sea* (Ikeda 1992), which did use the phrase. It turned out that the children discussed these books and used them as resources to raise minor issues and problems, but did not consider them in depth.

Because their inquiry had originated in the initial weeks of school some months earlier, the Seven Seas group was anxious to push forward. They decided to begin by writing to a museum to find out if Columbus's ship was still in existence. When they asked me what museum they should write to in Arizona I asked if they thought Arizona museums would have much information about ships and oceans. They opted to write to the Smithsonian, as it is a national museum. This group was the first in the class to write a letter. (The response was a long time in coming and offered little help, but the students were thrilled to receive an answer in the mail. After looking through the materials from the Smithsonian, they found that the information was more helpful to another group, so they passed the pamphlets on to them.)

While waiting for a response to their letter, the group revisited the Columbus books. They looked in the texts for places that Columbus had sailed and then went to the globe, locating the places and noting what seas were in the area. The children were somewhat frustrated using maps and globes. They found many bodies of water labeled "sea," and the name changes from the past to the present hindered their research. They took notes on their findings and made several trips to the library looking for more information, but interest dwindled with the lack of new leads about the seven seas. Finally, the group decided to try a new approach and headed for the telephone, calling the public library information line.

There was great excitement as they came back and reported to me that they had found out what today's world considers the seven seas. The surprise was that not all of these bodies of water had even been discovered at the time of Columbus, yet the term "sailing the seven seas" was already in use.

The students then decided that they would inquire about what people mean when they say "sailing the seven seas." They composed a form letter and used it as a survey, sending it to teachers, aides and spouses, the principal, several local boat businesses, and the local navy recruitment office. As they began to receive responses, I asked them what they were planning to do with the information. They hadn't thought about it, so we talked about different ways to record the incoming results of their survey. They decided to make categories and add tally marks to keep track of responses. Having worked with charts throughout the year, they easily incorporated this tool into their study (see Figure 3.3).

As we approached the end of the year, the Seven Seas group was influenced by a series of drama exercises and activities that they saw as part of our school's Arts in Education program. Choosing to create a mime presentation of the discovery of the seven seas, they used dramatic interpretation as another tool for relating their historical understandings. The group made a large world map on butcher paper with the help of an opaque projector and built a boat from classroom chairs and paper. They brought props from home and asked for little help, working independently and resolving their own problems as they arose. They also decided to continue their research on the meaning of "sailing the seven seas" by making a new version of their survey and passing it out to all the guests who attended our inquiry celebration. The children made a chart of their previous data for display. In their presentation, this group talked about the process of their research (as did all the groups). They explained their chart, pointing out the most popular responses as well as the ones they liked the best, such as the principal's comment that Seven Seas was a salad dressing.

I was impressed with the dynamics of the group. Debbie, the eight-year-old, was the leader and the primary recorder, but she was well supported by the other group members as they posed and solved problems, planned, and presented information. They applied many of the tools and strategies they already knew, such as consulting maps and globes, reading literature, and creating charts, and they tried new ones, such as writing letters and using pamphlets. There were no squabbles, and the group members respected one another. The result was a strong, collaborative effort from which the entire class benefited.

Figure 3.3
Seven Seas Chart

Another inquiry group, consisting of two eight-year-olds and a seven-year-old, asked, "What was Ms. Schroeder like when she was little?" This character study didn't seem to have much to offer in terms of inquiry; but, having worked so intently with the concepts of time and history, I thought there was potential in their question, especially since the teacher research group was realizing the importance of primary sources in studying history. At the group's initial meeting, I suggested they expand their question to include "What was the world like that Ms. Schroeder lived in when she was little?" They were agreeable to this added focus, feeling sure they were on to a really big scoop with their study!

To get this inquiry started I gave the group a set of books that were favorites of mine when I was young. Most were read-alouds, including *Caps for Sale* (Slodbodkina 1940), *Eloise* (Thompson 1955), *The 500 Hats of Bartholomew Cubbins* (Seuss 1938), *Cinderella* (Brown and Perrault 1954), and *The Story of Babar* (De Brunhoff 1933). I also included *Pompon* (L'Hommedieu 1955) and *The Winning Colt* (Floethe 1956), which reflected my love for dogs and horses; *The Secret Garden* (Burnett 1938), which was a significant reading accomplishment for me when I was a child; and *It's Not Fair!* (Harper 1986), which dealt with a middle-child syndrome for which I was famous. I did not expect the children to read all of these books. They browsed through this text set and concluded that I liked animals and adventure stories. Their next step was to go to the library looking for fictional stories set in the 1950s and 1960s and nonfiction texts about those decades.

As they read they began to write down specific questions about when I was young. I also encouraged them to ask questions about what it was like in the fifties and sixties. In brainstorming about how they were going to gather information, the group had said they were going to call my relatives. Since the members of my family all live on the other side of the country, I suggested that the postal system would be a more economical mode of communication. They immediately drafted letters to my father, my sister, and my brother. I helped edit and provided addresses, and the letters were off. Their letters included specific questions, such as "Was Ms. Schroeder funny when she was little?"

My mother had kept childhood artifacts, and I decided to share some of these with the inquiry group. I included a newspaper clipping of my kindergarten class, my kindergarten diploma, my first- and third-grade report cards, a report card mailing envelope that had a three-cent stamp on it, class pictures from third and sixth grades, and a picture taken when I was eighteen. The girls were thrilled with these, studying and asking questions about them.

Around this time I came across a book called *Close to Home* (Weaver 1993), a fictional account of the development of the Salk polio vaccine. It also described the political atmosphere in the early 1950s and the fear that enveloped the public about polio. I was particularly interested because my siblings and I were guinea pigs for the Salk vaccine. Both the center where the study was being conducted and my home town were mentioned in the book. I went back to my childhood artifacts and found my vaccination records on letterhead from the center. I gave the book to the girls. As they read it, one of them would periodically appear at my side and ask a question, such as "Is polio real?" I would provide an answer, the questioner would return to report to the group, and reading would continue. They also received responses from all three letters they sent. Both my father and my sister mentioned my strongly negative reaction to the vaccination testing experience, an extreme aversion to needles, confirming my participation in this historic event.

My family also sent photos from my childhood, insights into our family life, and stories about me. My father wrote mostly about my likes and dislikes as a child, my sister narrowed in on what I and our family life was like, and my brother focused on technology, noting that there were no microwaves, cable TV, computers, or CD players in our youth.

As the group received new information, they kept a list of questions that emerged so they could interview me. Unfortunately, we had not spent time talking about interviewing as a strategy and their questions were close-ended, making it a weak interview. However, the group felt they were getting good information.

One of the questions they kept asking was what music I listened to when I was young. I suggested that one place they might find out would be the local oldies radio station. They were extremely enthusiastic about this idea, but the radio station did not respond to their phone call. My aide suggested another resource might be a local restaurant, Little Anthony's Diner, which was modeled after a fifties youth hangout. After the group talked with the manager, they reported that two employees were eager to come to the classroom and talk about the 1950s. We set up a date and the two guests arrived, a woman in a poodle skirt and a man in a bow tie. They brought a few artifacts of the period, played the piano, had a bubble gum blowing contest, and taught the kids the hand jive, the hokey pokey, and the bunny hop.

As the group prepared their presentation of the results of their study, the girls decided to make a display board of the artifacts I had given them as well as the photos my family had sent. They took turns explaining the significance of each one. They described the encounter with the staff of Little Anthony's Diner, and they shared the book *Close to Home* (Weaver 1993), connecting it with the vaccination record. They also used their understanding of time lines to create a time line of my life, beginning with the information they had gathered on their own and adding more details they solicited from me. They gave an account of their learning process as well.

The Ms. Schroeder group had the advantage of having access to many primary sources for their study. Not only was I available on a daily basis; there was also my immediate family, who gave them firsthand accounts while offering different perspectives. The artifacts and photographs they had were real, rather than reproductions, and questions that came from studying them were addressed immediately. This inquiry was legitimate because it was well grounded in the authenticity of tools and resources. It even included a consideration of the worldwide threat of polio, for which the group had an artifact, my medical record, that was a primary source.

Our celebration of the discoveries the class had made through inquiry was held near the end of the year; parents, as well as some faculty, were invited. The audience was appreciative of the amount of time and effort the students had invested and could feel the sense of ownership and responsibility for learning that exuded from the children. We invited everyone to enjoy refreshments with us following all the presentations. It was a joyful occasion.

Looking Back over Time

My initial desire to develop a context for children to explore the concept of time led me to create opportunities for them to use the tools of historians and researchers. As I look back and reflect on the year, I realize that what I referred to as strategies at the beginning of the year were actually tools.

When we began thinking about history I provided the children with opportunities to become familiar with time lines, charts, and maps in the form of engagements—strategies, I thought, for understanding social studies. Later in the year the students worked in their inquiry groups and called on their new knowledge to carry out their plans. Because children had used time lines on a daily basis they understood them and could apply them appropriately to new situations. In the spring, after hearing a musical performance about how music from different times and places merged to form new styles, several students commented that it was like a time line of music. Time lines became a tool for better understanding many topics. Like strategies, tools need to be available in classrooms and demonstrated with children.

Students also began to understand the value of primary sources. When we read the many books on Columbus in the fall, the children found inconsistencies. They questioned where the information came from and how it could be different. The inconsistencies clashed with their concept of history, which was defined by truth and fact. For homework, children asked their parents what they had learned about Columbus in school, and, as they thought about the responses, the students recorded new questions, as Miranda did in Figure 3.4. Miranda's question, "Why did Dad's teacher

---

Christopher Columbus

What mom learned in school:

1. Columbus took away the Indians' home and killed them.

2. Columbus did not find India.

3. People thought Columbus was Spanish instead of Italian.

What dad learned in school:

1. Columbus sailed with three ships and never got where he was going.

2. Columbus thought the world was round and others didn't.

3. Columbus thought there was another way to get to India but there wasn't.

Differences
1. Dad talked about before Christopher Columbus got to the new work. I talked about after she got to the new world and mom talked about both. →

Questions
1. Why did dad's teacher teach him that the People thought the World was flat and they really knew it was round?

2. Why did Columbus sail with 3 ships?

Figure 3.4
Home Inquiry on What Family Members Were Taught About Columbus (Miranda, Age 8)

teach him that the people thought the world was flat and they really knew it was round?" triggered discussions about sources of information. These discussions, and the new understandings that followed, helped students form ideas and shape their thinking.

When primary sources were difficult to pursue or use in the classroom, the children sometimes altered their questions in ways that would enable them to gain access to firsthand accounts. For example, the bug group began looking at the history of bugs, but eventually focused on crop infestation. They found little to support their initial questions about the scientists who discovered the first bugs, but they were able to write directly to agriculturalists. Once these students realized that primary sources were possible to access, they preferred this more direct line to pursue their questions. Their search for resources took them into different knowledge systems, or disciplines, as they considered the questions and research sources of historians, paleontologists, scientists, and agriculturalists.

My own understanding of history, especially of primary sources, was reshaped during the year. While I had the advantage of knowing that issues are not always as they seem on the surface, I still assumed that history had but one interpretation. As a result of our classroom inquiry, my understanding of history is much broader now, and this has affected the way I represent historical issues in the classroom as a teacher. Recently, I reviewed Diane Stanley and Peter Vennema's book, *Cleopatra* (1994). In the front matter they note that all that is available about Cleopatra, all the primary sources, are written by her enemies. This little tidbit of information powerfully supports the idea that history is a collection of opinions and perspectives. How would Cleopatra's followers have portrayed her? Prior to working on this study, I doubt if a consideration of opinion or perspective would have played much of a role in my thinking about history.

Some students encountered another aspect of history that is not normally addressed in school. They became more aware of the significance history has in relation to the science and the future. The boys who examined the future of space found it necessary to back up and look first at the history of aviation. Their shift in focus began as they struggled with how they were going to get into space in order to explore and think about its future. In dealing with this question, they became engrossed with the history of aviation. They also had to sort through fantasy and factual accounts, and be able to differentiate between the two. Through this process they realized that to predict the future or to plan for it one needs to have an understanding of the past. History thus became a tool for thinking about the future.

Though we spent much time thinking about and discussing perspectives, I still have questions about my students' overall understandings. I wonder if they have internalized that they have the right to question a text. Will they apply what they learned about inquiry? Will they pursue primary sources on their own? Sometimes I fear the regimentation of school will squelch their attempts and dampen their spirits. Traditionally, children have been expected to answer questions in school, not ask them. As teachers we need to encourage both.

When looking at the past, teachers need to take on the role of researchers and ask children to do the same. In this way we help attain new perspectives and develop better understandings. We need to learn to think as historians and researchers and use their tools in posing and answering questions. We need to dig for primary sources to build our images and consider various points of view. We need to look at issues over time—in the past, in the present, in the future—and become aware of the dynamics that play out over time. Tools for exploring time can initiate and support many new inquiries.

Daily Schedule

7:55	Opening and class meeting
	Pledge, calendar, sharing
	Overview of the day
8:30	Workshop 1
9:45	Snack/P.E.
10:10	Workshop 2
11:00	Lunch
11:40	Independent reading and class read-aloud (read-aloud is often related to class inquiry focus)
12:20	Math workshop
1:10	Workshop 3

2:00   Closing

                Reflection on the day

                Glimpse of tomorrow

2:10   Dismissal

Workshops are blocks of time that can be used in many different ways to accommodate the negotiated curriculum. Workshops 1 and 2 include time for writing, reading, literature circles, strategy lessons, library research, and small- and large-group work. Workshop 3 typically includes whole-class work related to the class inquiry and short focused studies on other mandated curriculum topics.

There are no music, art, or physical education specialists in our schools.

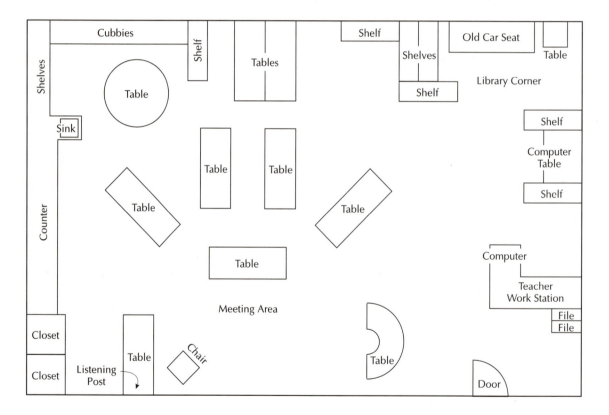

4 From 1492 to 1942: Gaining New Perspectives Through Literature

Gloria Kauffman

WAR AND PEACE
with a focus on personal conflicts

- "Getting to Know You" Interviews and Newspaper
- Sketch to Stretch Our Visions of Peace
- Strategies for Collaboration

- Engagements Around Concept of Discovery
- Discussions to Resolve Playground Conflicts
- Fall Interview

THE INDIAN IN THE CUPBOARD
with a focus on power

- Events That Have an Impact
- Effects of Time
- Changing Perspectives

- Learning from Change
- Recording Change

THE PINBALLS
with a focus on family stories

- Discussions of Abuse and Family Problems
- How to Change Our Lives
- Drawings of Home and Events
- Quilt Blocks

- Interviews with School Community
- How to Deal with Conflict
- Interviews with Family Members
- Family Poetry Books
- Personal and Family Time Lines

THE DEVIL'S ARITHMETIC
with a focus on culture

- Discussions of Time Travel
- Discussions of Culture

- Family Traditions and Celebrations
- Discussions About Religion

BOOKS ON COLUMBUS
with a focus on multiple perspectives

- Ownership and Bondage
- Changing Roles and Stereotypes
- Values, Beliefs, and Cultures

- Discovery vs. Invasion
- Harmony vs. Power

A FINE WHITE DUST
with a focus on rights

- *Mississippi Bridge*
- *To Walk the Sky Path*
- *Journey to Jo'Burg*

- *Shiloh*
- *From Slave to Abolitionist*
- *The Friendship and the Gold Cadillac*

GRAB HANDS AND RUN
with a focus on the denial of rights

ＦIFTH GRADERS can be exciting, and my class challenged me often as we planned curriculum that would be relevant to their needs and interests. Upon moving to Tucson I initially taught second grade, then fourth grade, which allowed me to follow my class of fourth graders to fifth grade. My new school was located in the southwest part of Tucson, and my class of twenty-four children came from many different ethnic backgrounds and socioeconomic situations. Even though most of the children moved with me to fifth grade, new children also joined our group, including a student who was visually impaired and did all of her work in braille.

While working with the curriculum, I had to keep in mind three audiences and their interests and perspectives. I had to ask myself, "What do my students need and want to study?" "What do I want to study?" and "What does the teacher research group want to study?"

My interest, along with the research group, focused on the students' historical and multicultural understandings of the events that surrounded Columbus and his "discovery" of America. The curriculum goals were to build a sense of historical understanding, to develop the students' concept of time, and to enhance awareness of multicultural perspectives. The students' interests would emerge throughout the year, but based on their age, I knew they would be concerned about themselves and how they were growing and changing emotionally and physically.

My goal was to create new understandings and an awareness of others through moving the students into an acceptance and appreciation of other cultures, using literature as a driving force. Stories of individuals, families, and culture could encourage discussion and reflection. Reading about others' hopes, fears, struggles, and triumphs would connect us across time and help us gain new perspectives on people's beliefs, thoughts, and actions in history and on the issues in today's world. We could add to these perspectives through our talk with each other, interviews, and other investigations.

In this chapter, I share our inquiry process and the decisions we made toward finding a class focus study. First I discuss the engagements we used to create community and to develop our class focus. I then take a closer look at the children's small-group research studies. Throughout the chapter, I focus on the role of literature in the inquiry process through our use of read-alouds, text sets, and literature circles (Short and Pierce 1990).

Creating Community and Developing Trust

The first week of school I planned many engagements to encourage children to become reacquainted with one another as well as to give new members of the class time to become part of the community. Throughout these curricular engagements, I challenged students to discover something new about each class member.

During the first week of school, we put together a class newspaper using the engagement Getting to Know You (Short and Harste, with Burke 1996). After generating interview questions together, the class broke into groups of two. The partners were to continue developing their own questions and, through interviewing, discover something new about each other. They recorded the information through notetaking and then wrote up the interviews and published a class newspaper. Ten-year-old Tino, for example, wrote about his interview partner, Yesenia:

> Meet Yesenia
>
> Yesenia is ten. She still is a little girl. She still needs a voice. She has six people in her family.
>
> In her spare time, Yesenia likes to play and watch TV. She likes to go to eat pizza. She likes her bike and her friends. She likes to go places to vacation. Her best travel was to San Diego. On holidays, she goes and visits her grandparents.
>
> Her favorite sport is kickball. Her personal interest is drawing. She likes to draw. Her favorite game is monopoly.
>
> Her birthday is April 4. She was born in Mesa. The color of her hair is brown and her eyes are brown. Her personality is shy, funny, polite, and smart.
>
> She treasures her ring.

We continued discovering new things about each other through reading with a partner, having class discussions, sharing family stories, and playing games together. We created individual name symphonies to introduce ourselves to each other through song, movement, and sound (Upitis 1990). Using graph paper and different colors for each letter in our name, we discovered diagonal, linear, or random patterns in our names. We created birthday books throughout the year by interviewing the birthday child and writing personal messages to that student, which were glued into a book and given to him or her.

During a brainstorming session at the beginning of the school year, ideas for looking at ourselves and others emerged. We continuously shared our ideas and concerns in order to build a collaborative community of learners in which we acknowledged our similarities and valued our differences. The fifth graders openly shared some of their concerns as we continued to build our community. They talked about the trouble they had getting along with their friends and family members and how they felt they didn't have control of their lives. Amber said, "I have too many privileges. I am having lots of fun. I need more boundaries from my parents. I get into too much trouble because I don't know when to stop. I am responsible but I don't want that much responsibility."

The students were growing up. They wanted the same privileges as adults, such as the ability to drive cars and stay out late, but they didn't want the responsibilities that went with these privileges. They shared how hard it was for them to learn to adapt to others and deal with new experiences. Their lives had changed through events such as a move to a new school, families' financial struggles, and parents' going back to school. "When I get mad at my parents, I take it out on my friends," stated Leola.

Students shared personal stories of how they found inner strength to deal with difficult times and how families come together to help each other survive. They were concerned about getting along with friends and family, understanding and trusting others, getting over shyness, talking about what they value, and finding and sharing their diversities. The subject of relationships with their classmates and others in their lives emerged as an inquiry focus for our class.

Merging the Class Interest and the Research Study

As part of the research study, the teacher research group had decided to record children's current understandings of history and perspective. We planned a fall interview to determine students' understandings at the beginning of the school year. My planning had to connect the interests of the students, myself, and the research study. The issue of whether children have rights emerged from our class focus on self. As we discussed how children get control of what they want to do, the concepts of power, freedom, and control seemed to interest the class and to offer a possible connection to the Columbus event.

To move our thinking forward and gain new perspectives about power, freedom, and control, I read *The Indian in the Cupboard* (Banks 1981) to the class. I understood the controversy over this book's stereotyping of American Indians as "wild savages." But I knew the book also highlights issues of ownership, the use of people as toys and caring for them as pets, children's manipulation of adults, and the moral obligations and responsibilities that come with power. I felt that this book was controversial enough to create discussion but that it also had depth and would relate to the research study of multicultural and historical understandings. The class read-aloud strengthened the children's discussion strategies and highlighted their understandings of issues.

For me, class discussions around picture books and chapter books are essential to establishing a supportive context for children's own inquiries. I carefully choose these read-alouds to offer new perspectives, challenge children's thinking, encourage personal connections, and demonstrate strategies they can use in their literature circles and inquiry groups (Smith 1990). As students work in small groups, I serve as a resource but do not join the groups to monitor or lead discussions. Instead, our class meetings and read-alouds are a time for the children to raise issues and demonstrate strategies through our talk together.

As I read aloud from *The Indian in the Cupboard*, we continued discussing issues of building trust, getting along with friends, and having control of our lives. We also discussed many of the ideas we had brainstormed from picture book read-alouds, adding new issues for future discussions. Questions about children's rights continued to be raised and the issue of effecting change through violent action emerged.

I then read aloud short stories dealing with the concept of peace from *Peace Begins with You* (Scholes 1990) and *The Big Book for Peace* (Durell and Sachs 1990) to provide perspectives on ways to take action. Whole-class discussions were not easy, so we used the curricular engagement of Sketch to Stretch (Short and Harste, with Burke 1996) to help focus our thoughts on what peace and power meant to each of us personally. Students drew sketches of their current understandings of peace and power. These sketches were shared in small groups and then with the whole class to open up children's talk about their personal experiences and connections. This sharing led to heated whole-class discussions.

Discussing these books on peace triggered memories of chapter book read-alouds from the previous year. Some children remembered books they had read in fourth grade on Hiroshima and World War II and asked me to bring them to class. These requests were a great opportunity for us to explore a class text set on Change over Time. I organized those books and other picture books into sets of six to eight dealing with issues of time and culture, based on issues raised in our class discussions: Events that Have an Impact, Effects of Time, Changing Perspectives, Learning from Change, and Recording Change. Small groups formed to read and discuss the sets. We always followed literature circles by sharing with the whole class and relating the small-group discussions to the whole-group focus of Changes over Time. It was also natural to relate our discussions back to the class read-aloud.

We kept a list of issues and questions that came up in our whole-class sharing and added to this list after each discussion. Questions included: Did the pilgrims and Indians have different ideas about the land? Why did the author do the research? How do people change? The issue of having and not having power seemed to dominate our discussions. We discussed rights and power as they played out among friends and in families. These class discussions led students to compare their family interactions with their interactions between friends.

Establishing the Class Focus

Students wanted to take time to discover how they fit into their families, how they built relationships with others, and how they could develop new ways of interacting in their family settings as they grew older. The issues generated through our small-group and class read-aloud discussions guided me in choosing the chapter book read-alouds. I think it is important for students to be able to make new connections with issues and questions they are already considering.

Our next chapter book, *The Pinballs* (Byars 1977), lent itself to a discussion of how one can interact with others and take ownership of one's own life while working together and valuing the family unit. (Figure 4.1 shows the web that resulted from *The Pinballs* discussions.) As our literature circles continued with the text sets on Change over Time, the class discussions focused more and more on issues of culture. John wondered, "Can you take someone's culture away from them?"

Pulling together the class discussions on self, the need to understand family traditions, and concerns about culture, religion, and power, I found a read-aloud that dealt with all these ideas. Over the next month, I read aloud *The Devil's Arithmetic* (Yolen 1988). This book helped us explore the question of losing one's culture as we continued looking at family interrelationships, heritage, and traditions. As we read, some confusion emerged about time travel, family traditions, and religion. Nannette pointed out that she lived in three cultures. She was Hopi when

Figure 4.1
*Class Web of Issues
from* The Pinballs
(Byars 1977)

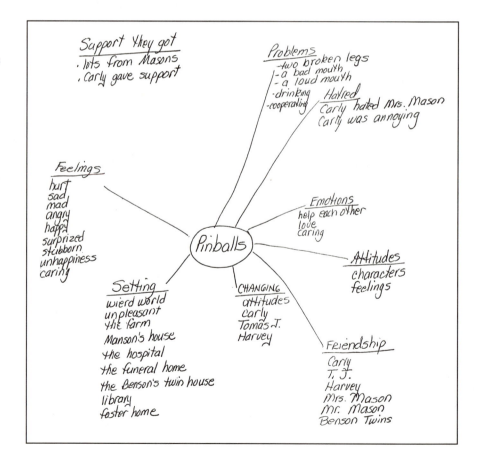

she went to Third Mesa for her naming ceremony, but she lived differently from her Hopi grandfather when she was at home in Tucson. In addition, she had to act, talk, and dress like her peers at school, which was different from the way she acted at home. As a result, she found it difficult to be herself because of her need to change roles for each situation.

As a teacher, I had planned engagements that I hoped would encourage students to connect to their own experiences. We learn by connecting to, and building from, our experiences. I had focused the curriculum on students' questions and the issues that concerned them. Through our class read-alouds, literature circles on chapter books, and text-set studies, we had time to talk, reflect, and gain an understanding of what we thought about issues that were important in our everyday lives. Through stories found in literature, we connected our own lives to those of people who lived long ago. We discovered concerns were similar across time and in all parts of the world. The hardships people suffered long ago were not that different from the hardships we suffer in our neighborhoods today.

Up to this point I had not introduced any books or discussion of the Columbus event. As part of the research study group I felt obligated to introduce Columbus, but I also wanted to emphasize the children's interests within our community of thinkers. It was difficult to find meaningful engagements to refocus the class on a new perspective without imposing my agenda. I thought if we looked at others who had stories similar to our own we might be able to expand our perspectives and understandings of history and culture. If we found anomalies, issues, and events we couldn't explain, we would generate questions.

I pulled together many versions, stories, and perspectives on the voyage and events that surrounded Columbus. We formed groups to consider various issues related to Columbus, and we started collecting information from as many sources as possible. We browsed, read, and discussed the books. We made time lines of the different versions of the events. We created a class chart on the similarities and differences found in the information across the books. We also made a mural from two perspectives, Columbus's and the Tainos Indians'.

These engagements gave students time for browsing through books, talking informally, discussing historical events, and gaining an understanding of this period in history. The sets of picture books gave us a quick overview. Students were somewhat confused by the differences in facts and the descriptions of Columbus, both in the written text and the illustrations. As learners we needed time to develop a context and time to find questions or issues that were worth spending time on as a class and as individuals.

During this time of gathering information I chose to read aloud some of the books in the text sets. *Encounter* (Yolen 1992) was one such book. Students were excited because Yolen was the author we were reading at chapter book time. They wanted to know if she always had a child sense danger and doom. Class discussions were exciting. Students started generating their own definitions of culture: "Culture is what you do." "Culture is your family's traditions." "Culture is your religion and what you believe." After much thought Nannette added, "Culture is in your heart, mind, and spirit."

One issue that disturbed the students was that Columbus took American Indians as slaves back to Spain. "At first I wasn't going to believe it when Bill said, 'Columbus had slaves sent to Spain.' I only believed that Columbus discovered America," said Rudy. The class couldn't understand that Africans were not the only slaves and that the Tainos culture was destroyed as a result of their enslavement. They wanted to know more about slavery. Another point of confusion arose from the read-aloud book, *The Devil's Arithmetic* (Yolen 1988). Arthur asked, "How can the same things be happening in 1492 and 1942?" He was beginning to understand the notion that history repeats itself, but was struggling with the idea that such similar events could happen five hundred years apart.

From our discussions concerning the Columbus events, we had many issues and questions. (The sentiments expressed in Rudy's reflection log, shown in Figure 4.2, were typical.) Drawing on the text sets we had brainstormed as a teacher research group, I put together sets from our class web of issues. Students signed up for a set of their choice, creating literature circles around Ownership and Bondage; Changing Roles and Stereotypes; Values, Beliefs, and Cultures; Discovery versus Invasion; and Harmony versus Power.

These text sets helped the class to find a focus for their inquiries. As groups discussed issues and then brought their major concerns to the class we found ourselves asking more questions dealing with rights. The browsing, or "wandering and wondering," of these sets led us to focus our questions around the subject of human rights. The class inquiry continued to concentrate on the mistreatment of people and the denial of their rights as human beings.

Collaborative Inquiry Groups

Students had a continuing interest in the rights of others (including animals), the rights of children, and especially their own rights. We decided to form interest groups that would begin researching the issues of the rights of African Americans, women, animals, and children. Other groups looked at the history of slavery and the issue of bondage today. One group became interested in legal and illegal immigration from Latin American countries and the growing population of refugees.

So much was going on in the room at the same time. I had to step back and reflect to understand where we had been and where we might be going. The focus on human rights stemmed from two sources. One was the students' concern for themselves personally, and the other was the literature study around the broad concept of Discovery. We started the year with looking at peace issues and solving problems together in order to live together harmoniously. We were exposed to different perspectives on the same issues when we studied the Columbus events. Many children wanted to explore their own issues, those of growing up and

Figure 4.2
*Reflection Log Entry
(Rudy, Age 11)*

> Christopher Clumbus
>
> I have so many doubts that I don't know weather to belive this imformation or not. because we don't know that Clumbus was true or any of this happened it's like on T.V you don't know if the product works or not

being caught between an adult world and a kid's world. They wanted to know more about the rights of people, especially children.

I continued to use literature as our main resource. I found stories of people throughout time and from various walks of life to deal with issues my students wanted to explore. Based on these major concerns we moved from the Discovery text sets into shared chapter book sets on rights. Groups signed up and read *Mississippi Bridge* (Taylor 1990), *To Walk the Sky Path* (Naylor 1973), *From Slave to Abolitionist: The Life of William Wells Brown* (Warner 1993), *Shiloh* (Naylor 1991), *The Friendship and the Gold Cadillac* (Taylor 1987), and *Journey to Jo'Burg* (Naidoo 1986).

There was also an interest in religion. Amber and Leola wanted to discuss their right to join the church of their choice and not the one their parents wanted them to join. Despite the chance of parental disapproval, I took a big risk and decided to read aloud *A Fine White Dust* (Rylant 1986). In this book, a preacher comes into a small town to hold revival meetings and sweeps up a young boy in the emotions of being saved. The boy wants to run away with the preacher, but learns that the preacher has left town with a young woman, betraying his newly found faith. Through this book we continued our discussions of religion and culture as a class while the inquiry groups began focused studies on the rights issue.

As students moved into their inquiries, they needed ways to collect and organize their ideas. They needed a place to think as well as preserve their new knowledge. We used literature logs, webs, charts, and time lines. We kept a running class list of questions along with individual lists in logs. I wrote lists of my own of issues, ideas, and connections in my field notes.

Inquiries on Rights

The inquiry groups emerged out of children's questions and interests about the rights of people and animals. I wanted to have the class focus on issues that connected us in some way so that we could continue talking together as a class. Issues, ideas, and misconceptions were dealt with on a much deeper level when the discussions were brought to the whole class after small groups had discussed their initial ideas. The students spent a great deal of time on their focused studies in their inquiry groups, but we met to share our ideas and to talk about our chapter book read-aloud in class meetings.

The inquiry groups began by reading a chapter book related to their inquiry focus and meeting as a literature circle. From these discussions, they moved into intensive investigation through interviews and primary sources. The *Shiloh* group spent most of their time discussing animal rights. They were upset at the abuse animals suffered because humans take out their frustrations on animals. The discussions centered around the abuse of children who then become adults who abuse. David's literature log entry, shown in Figure 4.3, reflects this group's concern. The group went on to contact various agencies for additional information.

The *To Walk the Sky Path* group spent time researching the Seminole people. The group was interested in their culture and what was kept and changed when Whites took their land. The students continued the discussion of how culture can be taken away from someone and were amazed that Seminoles welcomed and married runaway slaves. Indian land rights and the reasons for reservations were issues of concern to them. Through these discussions, Travis became interested in his own Apache background, and researched, wrote, and published a book on Apaches.

Figure 4.3
Literature Log Entry
(David, Age 11)

> Shiloh   Feb
>
> I think that starving an animal is not how you train a dog. My feeling for the book is sad because the way he gets treated. like for example getting kicked. around. Why does Judd even hit this dog? Dogs have rights too, I think that Judd lerned from his and it was passed down from Gerertion. I think that dogs are smart too.

Journey to Jo'Burg was a difficult book for the group. It was hard for the children to understand that people in South Africa were still separated because of color. They confused South Africa with the southern United States. Their research led them to further explore South Africa.

The *Gold Cadillac* group took a look at Black rights in the south. They talked about stereotypes of African Americans and interviewed children who had experienced prejudice. Amber talked about the prejudice and treatment she has experienced because of her blindness.

The *Mississippi Bridge* group spent most of their time talking about slavery and prejudice. They explored the issue of respect among African Americans and Anglos. John asked, "Wouldn't some problems be solved if Blacks respected Whites?" This question lead them to the library to research Black rights, slaves, and slavery. Rudy wanted to interview a slave; Arthur had an increasing interest in Black women and the strength they had to deal with slavery. Their discussions about Black women having more hope than Black men left John troubled. He couldn't agree with Arthur's statement "Women are stronger than men."

The group spent many hours in the library looking up Black rights. They found lots of information on slavery and abolitionists. They kept running lists of questions in their logs as well as comments about what they had read and maps of the Underground Railroad routes. Their lists of questions led to an interview with an African American teacher at the school. They also began reading magazines and newspapers for information on slavery in today's world.

I wanted the students to be open to other perspectives as they explored different issues. Because primary sources and original documents were scarce, it was difficult for us to take a historian's perspective. Most of the sources we had access to were reproductions of photographs and other people's interpretations of history. Such secondary sources often water down or withhold information from children. I wanted them to get beyond dates and facts. As inquirers, we needed to focus on the tools, processes, and perspectives of historians.

Children continuously shared what they were collecting and learning informally. Sharing their research findings more formally was a way to go public with what they knew and understood. Presenting ideas to the class gave them a chance to collect and organize their ideas and present them to others in a manner that made sense and communicated their understanding. It helped the children determine what they knew. It was also an opportunity for them to develop new questions and interests. As groups shared with each other, they offered others new invitations to learning.

For example, the Black rights group shared their initial questions and their library research on the history of Black rights. They talked to the class about their interview questions and shared excerpts from their taped interview with Mr. Foster, an African American teacher in the school.

Continuous reflection took place. Children looked at what they knew. The context of knowledge changed as they discovered new ideas. The process of digging through many sources and gaining many perspectives proved to be a challenge to most of the children. The answers were not just there, they had to be developed. Finally, why they were learning was made clear. We had a real purpose that led us forward in our learning and allowed individuals time to pursue their own questions.

After sharing their interview of Mr. Foster with the class, the Black rights group realized they themselves had not really listened to his answers to their questions. They had focused too much on asking the next question. Once they heard the taped interview they were able to go back and fill in the gaps by generating new questions. They discussed what they had done and planned their next steps.

As groups and individuals shared and listened to each other, new potentials for inquiry were created. The Black rights group became interested in the Buffalo Soldiers, a regiment of all Black soldiers during the Spanish American War. They found articles in newspapers and found that relatives of Buffalo Soldiers would be able to come to the classroom if they were invited. Leola wanted to know more about shelters for battered women. Amber was still concerned about whether or not she should join the church of her choice.

Continuing Inquiry

We began the year with engagements that encouraged students to become acquainted with one another in order for us to form a community of thinkers. Through the use of literature, students had many opportunities to use different strategies to collect and record data and look across time, thus growing in their understanding of diverse peoples.

Students read, discussed, thought together, and reflected on their perceptions of the actions and treatment of others in a variety of situations throughout time.

During all of these engagements we met often as a class to share information and discuss what we were learning about ourselves and each other. I took field notes on the interests I saw emerging to help me establish a class focus. From this focus, we could develop specific issues and questions through small-group inquiry studies and, eventually, personal inquiries.

Even though students had opportunities to pursue their individual interests and inquiries, I was interested in the studies a whole class and small groups might take on throughout the year as we looked at the concept of Discovery and as children stretched their thinking through the use of literature.

During wide reading and writing work time many students followed through with their own individual inquiries. Some became interested in Amish culture (this stemmed from the children's Indiana pen pals). Others wanted to look into their own ethnic backgrounds and cultures so they examined relevant topics, such as Apaches, life in Mexico, and life in Tonga. Other students' interests and research included Van Gogh's perspective of the world, braille, the role of gangs in Tucson, endangered animals, and people who educate themselves.

To build from our discussions of the denial of human rights, I read aloud *Grab Hands and Run* (Temple 1993), the story of a family fleeing from Guatemala to Canada because of political reasons. This book ignited an interest in refugees and visiting sanctuaries in the Tucson area. Students wanted to talk to refugee families and collect stories. Unfortunately, the end of the year arrived, putting an end to our inquiry at school.

Reflecting on the Year

All year long our class created a community based on trust and communication. We spent the year exploring issues that developed from the interests of the students, the concerns of the teacher, and the questions of the teacher research group. Our goal was to create new understandings and an awareness of others through acceptance and appreciation of other cultures.

Using literature as the primary method for understanding individuals, families, and diverse communities enabled the class to reach new understandings and ask more questions dealing with the equality of all people. Students met and discussed the past and related their own life experiences to past events.

Literature enabled us to step into the shoes of others; to become those people and know how they faced problems. We were able to gain insight into everyday events and how people dealt with world issues on a daily basis.

Through class discussions, students learned to build on each other's comments and share personal opinions. Issues that came up in class discussions helped me choose a class read-aloud to address the students' concerns but also to raise new issues.

Concepts and themes in the books read during literature circles related to the chapter book read-aloud. Students referred to their own literature circle discussions during class discussions. As the students shared their connections, the class was kept informed of new and differing perspectives on similiar issues. In accepting our similiarities but facing our problems we had a firsthand example of how people of different beliefs can live together.

The end of the year ended our formal inquiry, but we learned that inquiry never needs to end. The questions and research continue with each child's own interests.

Daily Schedule

8:00	Reflection journals
	Quiet time for writing about life outside school
	Attendance, lunch count
8:30	Class meeting
	Sharing journals
	Schedule for the day
	Class and school business
9:00	Reading work time
	Literature circles
	Response to literature across sign systems
	Wide choice reading

Partner reading with different strategies

Inquiry groups

10:15   Free writing time

Free choice writing

Class projects

Pen pal letters

Authors circles

Inquiry groups

Publish books

11:30   Chapter book read–aloud

Related to the inquiry focus

Whole class discussions—connect book to inquiry groups

12:00   Lunch

12:40   Work time

Math strategies/P.E./computers

Inquiry groups

Class studies related to other mandated curriculum topics

2:00   Dismissal

The three work times are interchangeable depending on children's needs and the projects they are working on.

Friday mornings from 8:30 to 12:00 is studio.

There are no music, art, or P.E. specialists in the school.

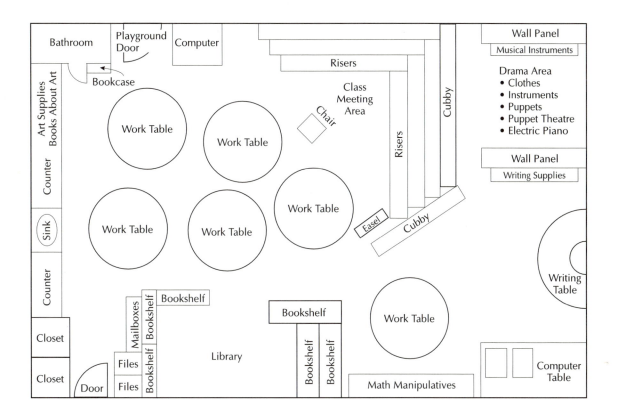

5 Should We Let It Fizzle and Blow Up? Examining the Inquiry Process Through Focused Studies

Kathleen Marie Crawford

FAMILY/SELF-DISCOVERY

- Mean Parents
- Stepparents
- Brothers and Sisters
- Sisters
- Brothers

- Family Quilts
- Science/Art Experiments
- Fall Interview
- "Getting to Know You" Interviews and Newspaper

CHRISTOPHER COLUMBUS FOCUS

- Ownership
- Discovery
- Stereotypes
- Journey
- Harmony with Nature

- Greed
- Change over Time
- Revisiting Columbus Books
- Inquiry Groups on World War II, Environment, and Space

ARIZONA/NATIVE AMERICAN AWARENESS

- Arizona History
- The Apache People
- Cesár Chavez

- The Navajo People
- The Hopi People
- American Indian Boarding School

MULTICULTURAL AWARENESS

- *Mississippi Bridge*
- *The Green Book*
- *Tuck Everlasting*
- *Number the Stars*
- *Roll of Thunder, Hear My Cry*

- *Dragonwings*
- *The Pinballs*
- Inquiries on Civil Rights, Foster Children, Divorce, Jewish Culture, and World War II

THE JUST TREATMENT OF ALL PEOPLE

- Individual Inquiries by Students

- Portfolio Reflections

WHEN KAREN and her mother came to visit the classroom a week before school started, we talked about her summer vacation and what we would be doing in fourth grade. She had been to Washington, D.C., and had visited an exhibit on the Columbus quincentenary. Since our broad theme of Discovery had come out of the Columbus issue, I wondered how Karen's knowledge might lead us in new directions in future conversations. I had taught Karen and ten of her classmates in first grade, so we already had a relationship from which to begin our conversations in fourth grade. All thirty-three students were from the southwest part of Tucson and had diverse cultural and socioeconomic backgrounds.

In this chapter, I describe how we came together as a classroom to explore the process of inquiry. The initiating experiences around the broad concept helped us establish a sense of community and introduced the inquiry process. I highlight the decisions we made as a class as we moved through inquiry for the first time, along with my struggles to listen to students' questions. Focused studies helped students engage in inquiry to form understandings about culture and different perspectives.

Creating Community

To encourage students to discover each other and think about their processes of learning, I planned several engagements to facilitate our getting to know and understand each other. We began the year by brainstorming a web of what Discovery meant. Students' responses varied from "discover America," "new lands," and "new stars" to names of inventors, such as Thomas Edison and Alexander Graham Bell.

The ideas on the web led to a class mini-focus on Discovery to explore the broad concept further and to get to know each other better. Students worked in pairs to discover what happens when watercolor paint is sprinkled with salt or rubbing alcohol onto a wet picture. Carlos and Samuel thought it would "fizzle and maybe blow up." They explored the reaction of water and alcohol by putting different amounts of each on the paper to see the effects. The students were beginning to work with each other as well as learn about their partner. This learning was extended into a class newspaper through our use of the engagement Getting to Know You (Short and Harste, with Burke 1996). Students paired up, and each discovered something about the other by creating questions that others might be interested in knowing about their partner. In addition to writing an article, students used this information for class graphs on birthdays, favorite colors, books, and hobbies.

We highlighted the discovery process throughout all our activities for the first couple of weeks of school. While playing softball, we discovered how to treat members of our team and other teams with respect. We changed the rules of the game so all students had a chance to run the bases. This was not easy for students who were used to seeing things from only one perspective, their own. Some of the students discovered what it felt like to make a home run. Charles, who had never had the opportunity to play in a team sport, was cheered on by his classmates as he ran the bases for the first time.

I introduced a focus on self-discovery and family history to support students in thinking more about the broad concept through their personal understandings of family. Students chose a family story from the many books displayed in the room to read and discuss with a partner. We shared the books with the class in an informal setting by having the partners give book talks. The partners talked about what they noticed in the book, what it reminded them of, and how the book made them feel (Kelly 1990). These strategies were used to encourage students' oral and written response to literature. After each group shared their book with the class, we sorted the fifteen books into groups. The students came up with six categories, including books about sisters, brothers, brothers and sisters, stepparents, mean parents, and family quilts. We used these categories to make text sets. The students then chose the text-set discussion group they wanted to join. Each group found several more books from the classroom and school library that they felt fit into their text set. I was interested to see how the students would talk about the literature in their groups and whether they would find a focus for further inquiry through these discussions.

For many of my students this discussion on text sets of family books was their first time in small-group literature circles. They needed a demonstration of what literature circles look like and how they function. As students met in their groups, we held class meetings to discuss what they would do next in their literature circles. The class suggested time limits and ideas for what they might talk about in their groups. We spent several days reading the books, then a few more days webbing ideas from the books and organizing the web to support their discussions.

The group on mean parents cut their web apart and put the words or phrases into categories they created. One pile contained words, such as greedy, mean, selfish, jealous, hurt, and demanding; other piles had ideas, such as making bad decisions and having mixed-up feelings. The students used these piles as tools to help facilitate new discussions and inquiries around these topics.

The students discussed questions and issues they wanted to explore instead of waiting for me to provide questions to answer as in previous years. After a couple of weeks of reading and discussing, students presented the ideas they had explored in their groups. Some of the groups had issues they wanted to examine with the class, such as divorce, getting along, and problems with brothers and sisters. Other groups just wanted to retell the books through plays. Because I had asked the groups to report on their discussions up to that point, some groups did not have an extended time to reflect on their work in greater depth. I saw this first set of literature circles as providing a demonstration of how literature circles function and so did not extend the groups over time into more in-depth discussions. I wanted the students simply to have an understanding of the process of talking in groups and finding topics they could connect to as we moved into other inquiry experiences.

As we participated in literature circles, the students made individual time lines of their lives. The concept of time was an easy topic for these fourth graders to understand, so I decided to introduce books focusing on Change over Time that were part of a text set that our teacher research group had developed. I felt my students would benefit from whole-group literature discussions before going into another small-group experience. Diane, my student teacher, and I read aloud *The Sandal* (Bradman 1989), *A Penny in the Road* (Precek 1989), *Window* (Baker 1991), *Where the Forest Meets the Sea* (Baker 1988), *The House on Maple Street* (Pryor 1992), and *Yonder* (Johnston 1988) in a three-day span as the class talked about the connections, issues, and concerns these books elicited.

The students quickly picked up on the connection between time and change in these books. I knew we needed to move on, but I did not know how to work with my students in making decisions about where to go next. I didn't have a clear enough understanding of a connection between change over time and the students' questions to figure out how to move forward. I didn't allow enough time for students to wander and wonder so they could find their own issues and questions and make their own connections. I was trying to find their connections for them instead of giving them time to find their own connections and negotiate the focus of the curriculum. It wasn't until later that I realized that students need plenty of time to wander and wonder in areas they want to explore further in order for them to find and pursue their inquiry questions.

Introducing the Inquiry Process

One of the main planning-to-plan activities of our teacher research group involved pulling together text sets on issues we thought might come out of the broad focus of Discovery in our classrooms. We spent a great deal of time gathering and purchasing books that would fit into the different text sets we developed around Discovery. We had also initially set a time limit for our research project. Columbus Day was right around the corner, and I knew that in order to somehow keep to our time limit, I needed to jump into the text sets. To help make a connection between change over time and these sets, I read many Columbus books to the students: *Encounter* (Yolen 1992), *All Pigs on Deck* (Fischetto 1991), *I, Columbus* (Roop and Roop 1991), *Pedro's Journal* (Conrad 1991), and *The World in 1492* (Fritz 1992).

Although we discussed each book separately, we did not take time as a class to find and connect the ideas to our own issues. Instead, I pulled out seven of the text sets our teacher research group had developed that I thought were related to my students' discussions. I should have given more time for the students to explore, talk about, and reflect on the books as a whole, and then we could have organized them into text sets together based on the issues they were finding significant.

The sets I thought related to issues in their initial discussions were Ownership, Stereotypes, Greed, Discovery, Journeys, Harmony with Nature, and Changes over Cultures. These text sets, of five to fifteen books each, were put out for students to browse for several days. Most students showed an interest in the new books and they noticed that some of the family and Columbus books from our earlier discussions were in the sets. This led to a discussion about when it is OK to read a book more than once. After browsing, the students wrote down the text sets in order of preference for the group they wanted to join. Students were given their first or second choice. The children met in their groups an hour each day for a week to read and take notes on the books. Through literature logs, webs, and sketches, they made connections to the books and identified issues to discuss.

During this week of reading, I began a whole-class discussion on the set of books that was not chosen, Change over Cultures. Diane and I read these books to the students and asked them to write down issues and concerns related to the books. They talked in groups of three or four and then shared their ideas with the whole class. We wrote down their ideas on a large piece of butcher paper as we read through each of the seven books in this set. As a whole class we tried to find a focus from this set of books. Having a common text set to explore together provided the students with a demonstration of how they might go about talking in their groups. I also hoped these discussions might help us find an inquiry focus for the whole class.

Framing Inquiry Through Focused Studies

About this time Carolyn Burke (1992) came to Tucson for a presentation on using "focused studies" to plan a curriculum. I liked Burke's framework for inquiry and felt my students would have a better idea of where they were going in their small groups if they had an overall sense of the process we were using. I adapted Burke's structure and presented it to the entire class in the context of the Changes over Cultures text set we were discussing as a class.

1. What issues and concerns are you interested in studying?
   —Talk with others.
2. Choose a topic.
   —List what you believe about it.
3. What do we want to find out about the topic?
4. What do we have available for the research?
   —Sources: books, interviews, media, etc.
5. Take notes on the research.

99

6. Create invitations related to your research.
7. Reflect on the research.
8. How will we share our experiences?

We looked at our chart paper of issues and concerns from the Change over Cultures text set and decided it was similar to the question "What issues and concerns are you interested in studying?" We then decided to find significant issues common to the books in the text sets. We listed five, and later narrowed these down to one: the issue of separation. We talked about what we believed about this issue and narrowed the topic further to kidnapping and why someone would kidnap another person. The students brainstormed how resources and tools could be used to examine this issue and came up with interviewing police, family members, and the victim; reading books, newspapers, encyclopedias, and magazines; and watching the news on TV. I told the students that this was the beginning of a study we could pursue and that what we had just done was a demonstration of what they could do in their small groups. Alejandro commented, "Oh, this makes sense. Now I see why we're webbing out the different issues of the books."

At this point, the students seemed to have a better understanding of where they were going as they explored their text sets to find a possible focus for inquiry. However, I still felt that some students did not feel enough of a sense of ownership in the process. I asked the groups, "What are you doing?" and "Why are you doing it?" From their answers I could tell that three out of the six groups had a clear focus. The student teacher, Diane, and I decided to have the three groups who lacked focus revisit the Columbus books so they could pull out their own issues and concerns. We realized that we had pushed our own issues through the text sets and had not given the students time to find their own.

The three groups that had found a focus changed their group names from the text set of books they were reading to the inquiry focus in which they were interested. The Ownership text set group wanted to look at pollution and its effects on Earth. They read *The Green Book* (Walsh 1982), which takes place in the future when a small community needs to leave Earth because of the pollution that has occurred. Some of the group's notetaking came through observations and discussions of pollution in their own lives. They studied their neighborhood desert and discussed ways to clean up the environment in the community. They also talked about how their families recycled in their homes.

The group that began with the text set on Discovery decided to look into war. They chose World War II for the focus of their inquiry, and they read *Number the Stars* (Lowry 1989), so that they might begin with a common understanding. (Figure 5.1 shows the web they developed after reading this book.) They talked about the problems of war and why Jewish people were treated so badly during World War II. They also wondered how people who fought in the war felt about the battles. Carlos

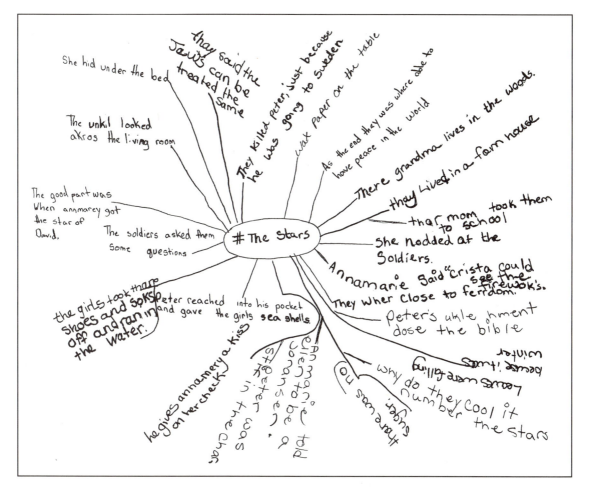

Figure 5.1
Inquiry Group Web on Number the Stars *(Lowry 1989)*

interviewed his grandfather, who had fought in World War II, for answers to some of his initial questions. This group also spent time at the school library using informational books on World War II.

Another group, Harmony with Nature, had questions about the human causes of disaster, so I gave them *Sadako and the Thousand Paper Cranes* (Coerr 1977). This group touched briefly on the effects of the atomic bomb that was dropped on the city of Hiroshima in Japan, but they were more interested in the art of paper folding. They found several books on origami to learn how to make paper cranes. Ronald commented to his group, "After we learn how to make them, maybe we can make a thousand paper cranes!" Christine said, "Maybe we can make a center for everyone else to make them also and one of us stay there to help others make the cranes." This group seemed to lose their way, contenting themselves with a "cute" project instead of dealing with the original focus of their inquiry.

In a presentation at the University of Arizona, Karen Smith (1992) talked about setting up an environment for inquiry. She stated that teachers need to utilize all the spaces available to them in schools, in and out of their own classroom. I saw the need for students to have places where they could work with all the different research sources available. With thirty-three students in one room, I knew I needed to take advantage of other places in my school. Small groups of students went with my teaching assistant and Diane (who carried a tape recorder so as not to miss what happened in the small groups) to the library and conference rooms in the school to discuss and research their topics. These spaces created quiet places for the small groups to have uninterrupted, in-depth conversations. The students discussing World War II wanted to find a place where they could quietly read, then discuss what they read. They chose to move their group to a corner of the library that had a large, open area.

The students who did not have a focus came together as a large group to revisit the Columbus books and to look at different perspectives of the Columbus event. Originally we had planned for them to explore the books and then form several small groups based on their issues. However, they remained one large group that stayed together with Diane and explored their questions because they were so interested in why Columbus and his men mistreated the people they met. Through the conversations about the Columbus books, these students explored the unjust treatment of other people. They also gained a better understanding of the inquiry process by working with Diane in a large group.

Through participating in these focused studies, students realized that their thinking and opinions mattered and were listened to by others. They talked more about their learning processes than any other group of students I have taught. Josh commented, "I see. So we can keep on studying the issues we want to, and it just keeps continuing as we look at new things?" This was a major breakthrough for this child, because he had resisted the idea of the inquiry process when it was first presented to the class. He came to realize the value of working on issues that were important to him. The class worked through the process of a focused study and gained an understanding of the inquiry process.

Through the students' interest in the Columbus issues, they became aware of different perspectives on Columbus and wanted to find out more about the people who were in America before Columbus. Because Arizona history, geography, and culture are part of our district's fourth-grade curriculum, I was able to connect the children's interest in the people that lived in Arizona before Columbus to the district's mandates. They chose to look at the Apache, the Navajo, and the Hopi peoples. They asked about the culture of these groups, such as the purpose behind the different dances, styles of jewelry, and ways of hunting. They looked at the treatment of children in American Indian boarding schools as well as activists, such as Cesár Chavez. The students' inquiries on American Indians in Arizona led them to an interest in the treatment of people from many different cultures.

Accepting Different Cultures

Because the class wanted to look at the cultures of various groups of people, I introduced seven chapter books that dealt with the treatment of people of different cultures: *The Pinballs* (Byars 1977), *Mississippi Bridge* (Taylor 1990), *Roll of Thunder, Hear My Cry* (Taylor 1976), *Dragonwings* (Yep 1975), *Number the Stars* (Lowry 1989), *The Green Book* (Walsh 1982), and *Tuck Everlasting* (Babbitt 1975). Those of us who had read the books gave book talks. Students were eager to choose their books and move into literature circles to discuss different cultures. For many students this would be the first chapter book they had ever read. Sean, who was receiving special support services for his reading, asked another student in his group to help him get through the book. He felt secure enough to risk asking for help from his peers because he was accepted in our class.

Once the students formed groups, they met to negotiate among themselves how and when to read the books. Most groups met on a daily basis while reading the book. After all the members in a group finished reading, they talked about their initial reactions to the book. They brought their literature logs with them for support in their conversations if needed. After the first discussion students wrote about their thoughts, concerns, and questions before the next meeting. At that meeting several groups used webs to organize their thoughts as they shared their ideas and talked them through with group members.

Each group focused their discussions on an issue related to their book. The group reading *The Pinballs* focused on the unjust treatment of foster children. They began their sessions by talking about the characters and the way they were treated. In order to get to an understanding of how the characters might have felt, this group spent many sessions talking about the feelings of foster children. In our class we had two students who were living with foster parents. They became primary resources for information on what it was like to live in a foster home. The presentation the group eventually put together to share with the class consisted of interpretive drawings of how the three main characters in *The Pinballs* felt before and after entering the foster home. (Figure 5.2 shows an example of their work.)

After their presentation, the group began a new inquiry about children's rights. Claire and Elise were concerned about how children can avoid abuse. They questioned how children were placed in foster homes and called the Child Protective Agency to find answers. They discovered that they needed to learn notetaking when they found that adults talk faster than they could write. The girls also asked for literature from the agency to inform them about children's rights. Elise thought deeply about this issue. "When you get abused," she said, "you're like a bee and you get mad. This [group] helped me understand that people do care for abused children . . . sometimes they [abused kids] may not think anyone cares but it's not true, everyone does because I asked everyone in our class and they all said they do care."

The group of students who read *Roll of Thunder, Hear My Cry* talked about the unjust treatment of African Americans in the South. Their literature logs and webs had questions and issues that came from the book, such as, "Why can't Black people have White friends?" "Why did they [White people] 'whoop' them [Black people]?" "There were lots of accidents."

Figure 5.2
The Pinballs
Presentation (Elise and Claire, Age 10)

"Why did the Ku Klux Klan burn the land?" The group wanted to understand the different ways people are treated based on the color of their skin. Their inquiry became "to find out about other cultures and how they were raised." American Indians, Latinos, Anglos, and African Americans were the four groups they decided to study. They used their webs and logs as tools to think through why people of color are treated differently. (Figure 5.3 shows a typical literature log entry from this group.)

Students conducted interviews with several people from each ethnic group. They interviewed teachers, parents, and the principal at our school and asked them about what it was like growing up in their particular communities. The students brainstormed a list of people they wanted to interview and then realized they needed to set up a schedule for the interviews. Originally they had just a list of names of school personnel; they did not know when and how to make a schedule for the interviews. We made a list of the times when these students could be out of the room, and they used this list to schedule the people they wanted to interview.

One of the students typed up the interview questions and made copies for each person they wanted to interview. The questions were: "How did you get treated by different cultures when you were little? If

Figure 5.3
Literature Log Entry
(Claire, Age 10)

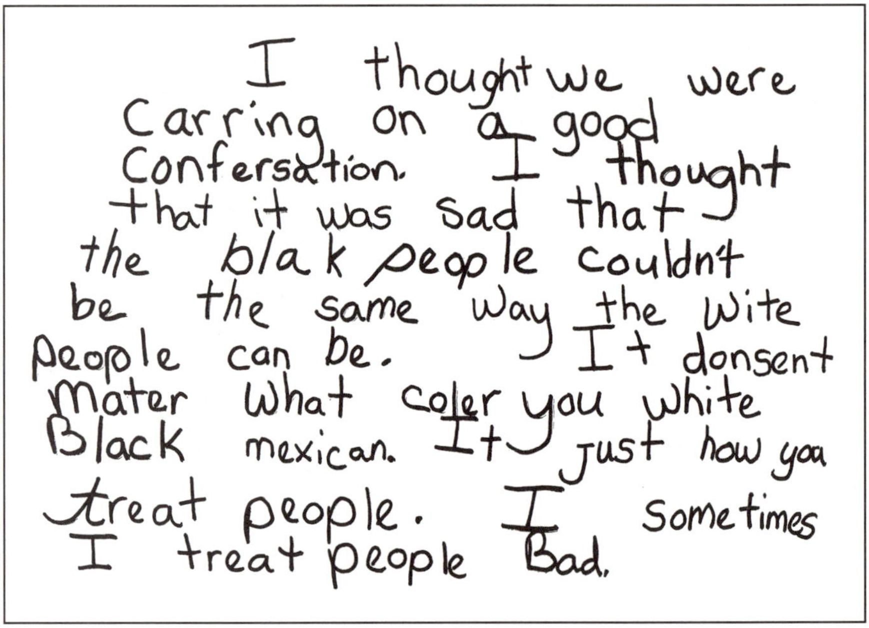

I thought we were carring on a good confersation. I thought that it was sad that the blak people couldn't be the same way the wite people can be. It donsent mater what coler you white Black mexican. It just how you treat people. I sometimes I treat people Bad.

you were threatened by different people in what way did it make you feel? What did you feel when this was happening? and why? How would you respond to this poem?" During the interview, they read a poem from *Roll of Thunder, Hear My Cry* and asked the interviewee to respond.

The group reading *Mississippi Bridge* looked into civil rights. They wanted to know about Malcolm X, John F. Kennedy, and Martin Luther King, Jr. Charles, an African American student in this group, was able to provide information to the other four boys about Malcolm X and Martin Luther King, Jr. He gained the respect of his group members because of his expertise on civil rights, which he had learned from his parents. Mike commented that he didn't realize how much Charles knew. Mike and Charles had not previously shown respect for each other, but by talking and sharing information, a new kind of understanding began to take place. Their mutual respect carried over to other parts of the school day, not just within their literature discussions.

Other groups in the class discussed religion as culture and family culture. The discussions from their literature circles led to serious whole-class discussions on the way we treat people. Their concerns about behavior in the lunchroom, playground, and hallways carried over from our class talks. They became much more aware of the needs of other people and not just their own needs. The students seemed to treat each other with more respect and acceptance.

Students as Expert Inquirers

As the focus on accepting other cultures came to a close, students asked for time to explore specific topics that they were interested in. We had kept a chart of questions we did not have time to explore during our focused studies throughout the year. Students revisited the chart, formed new questions, and decided to work alone or in small groups to explore their concerns in expert projects (Smith 1992). They examined a tremendous range of topics, including Jewish culture and religion, child abuse, the Bermuda Triangle, ocean tides, sharks and other animal life in the ocean, mythology, Greek and Roman gods, the Ku Klux Klan, China, and Pele.

Students chose these topics carefully to reflect issues that were important in their lives or interests that they wanted to pursue. Samuel, who is Jewish, decided to research his own religion. In previous years he had been teased about his religion by other classmates. But in this safe setting, which we had created through dialogue and learning to accept other perspectives, he shared the traditions of his family and religion with the members of his class. Mike, who was fascinated by the 1960s, looked into the assassination of President Kennedy. He brought his understanding of the civil rights movement from the discussions of *Mississippi Bridge*; now he wanted to examine a particular event during that time period.

Reflections

When I began this project, I looked at our teacher research time line as a framework I needed to follow. But by listening closely to my students, I learned that within a curriculum based on inquiry, children need time to discover questions and issues of importance. My students eventually were provided with time to explore their own questions. I came to understand their needs by living through the process with them. Their questions grew out of personal reflections on the focus topics, not from my pre-planned engagements. My students and I learned that time must be devoted during the school day for exploring and discussing our own issues and concerns on the topics under consideration.

The focused study model that Carolyn Burke presented changed my understanding of what the process of inquiry can look like in the classroom. My students' beliefs about inquiry became clearer as we deepened our understandings by working through a focused study as a whole class. Because we felt more secure about the inquiry process, we were able to open ourselves up through personal reflection and group discussion.

The students gathered available resources from school and home. They discussed their responses to literature, and used the voices in literature as a way of knowing the world around them. They interviewed people about topics of interest to have a better understanding of different perspectives on the same topic. They made their own observations about issues in their own lives. They tried to pull information from many areas to create new understandings of their topics.

As the students gathered information on topics that they were concerned about, they used strategies to help them record their data. They expressed an interest in notetaking as a result of their phone and personal interviews, they learned to scan books as they read for information, and they developed discussion strategies. Formal presentations gave students a chance to share understandings from their focused studies. The students became experts on their topic and by sharing gave other students a view of what their classmates were interested in.

As the students wrote final reflections on their individual inquiries at the end of the year, they had new questions to pursue. They learned that the inquiry process "keeps going and going," thus allowing them to explore their own interests. They understood that they can question the information they read.

By using a broad concept within the framework of the inquiry process and focused studies, the students gained an understanding of one another's cultures and came to appreciate the diversity of all people. Instead of one voice dominating our classroom, we learned to hear many perspectives and to appreciate our diverse community as we worked together in our shared goal of learning about the world and our own lives.

Daily Schedule

8:00	Learning logs: reflection on current understandings of class focus
8:20	Class meeting (student-led): attendance, lunch count, joys and sorrows, current events, and sharing of learning logs (5–6 per day)
8:50	Work Time I: Focus on learner as reader. May include read-alouds, quiet reading, literature groups, inquiry groups, shared/partner reading, writing workshop, individual inquiries
10:30	Math strategies or other mandated curriculum topics not incorporated into class focus inquiries
11:30	Lunch
12:10	Chapter book read-aloud related to inquiry focus
12:30	Work Time II: Focus on learner as writer (2–3 days a week). Quiet writing, writing groups, reading to support writing, publishing, or continuation of morning work time Fine art focus (2–3 days a week). Music, art, drama, P.E.
1:40	Class meeting: Evaluate day as a class through discussion of new learnings and new understandings

Learning Together
Through Inquiry

2:00   Dismissal

There are no music, art, or P.E. specialists in our school. Teachers teach all these areas.

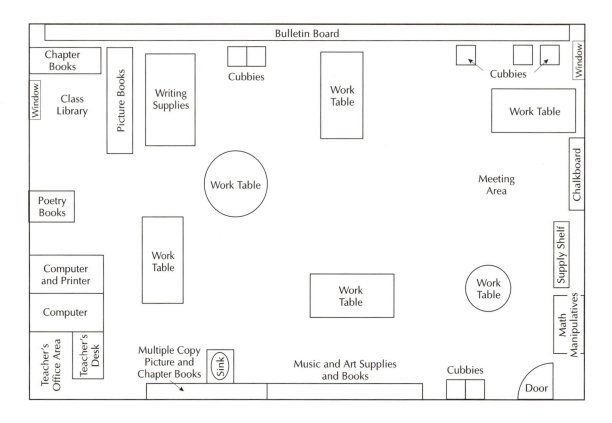

6 Stories, Trees, Time Lines, and Islands: Pursuing Children's Questions Within Predetermined Curriculum

Margaret J. Ferguson

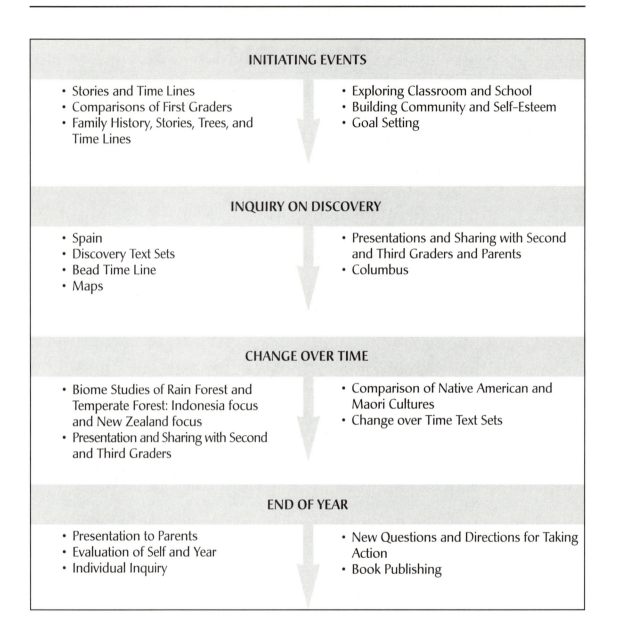

INITIATING EVENTS

- Stories and Time Lines
- Comparisons of First Graders
- Family History, Stories, Trees, and Time Lines

- Exploring Classroom and School
- Building Community and Self-Esteem
- Goal Setting

INQUIRY ON DISCOVERY

- Spain
- Discovery Text Sets
- Bead Time Line
- Maps

- Presentations and Sharing with Second and Third Graders and Parents
- Columbus

CHANGE OVER TIME

- Biome Studies of Rain Forest and Temperate Forest: Indonesia focus and New Zealand focus
- Presentation and Sharing with Second and Third Graders

- Comparison of Native American and Maori Cultures
- Change over Time Text Sets

END OF YEAR

- Presentation to Parents
- Evaluation of Self and Year
- Individual Inquiry

- New Questions and Directions for Taking Action
- Book Publishing

OUR CLASSROOM focus on Discovery began before school started. I sent each student a letter inviting him or her to come to school on registration day to get acquainted with me, the classroom, and the Discovery focus. The letter explained that all first graders were invited to "hop into first grade to discover" and had a rabbit drawing on it. This rabbit became our symbol for discovery. The letter also included a request for students to bring in a picture they had drawn of something they had discovered during the summer. These creations would become our first discovery bulletin board. Students would be asked to explain what they had made, why, and what materials they had used to create their picture.

Most of the students were able to come to school on registration day to explore the classroom. They chose a desk and participated in discovery centers. These activities included making a name plate for their chosen desk, creating a rabbit holding a sign about something they wanted to discover during the school year for our hallway bulletin board, placing their discovery pictures on the classroom bulletin board, predicting and recording whether they thought they could improve on the previous class's record for the number of books read during the year, creating a cover and putting together a personal journal, and finding a way to share the fourteen cubbies among the twenty-seven students.

The activities encouraged students to get involved, talk to each other, and move around the classroom so they could become familiar with the materials and physical setup of the room in a nonthreatening way. Parents helped their children work through the tasks and had some of their own to complete (filling out family reading interest surveys and classroom volunteer forms, signing up to provide snacks, learning procedures for keeping track of books read to or by students at home, looking through the first weekly newsletter, and reading ideas for gathering items for the weekly math guessing jar). I made a video of students and parents and took pictures for the class photo album to begin our class history. I also introduced students to each other and talked to them about their interests and expectations.

So began the preparation for an exciting year, a year of hard work and learning by the students and their teacher. This chapter highlights the history of that year; the journey the students and I went through together as we developed and refined the broad concept of Discovery using the inquiry cycle as a framework. Throughout the year, there were many changes in the curriculum and in my role as I tried to fit the inquiry cycle into a predetermined social studies curriculum I had created with a parent volunteer and two other teachers at my school. Students' roles changed as more ownership was given to them and as they tried to fit together and pursue the predetermined curriculum along with their own inquiry questions.

Exploring Discovery as a Classroom Community

On the first day of school, students came in eager and ready to start because of their experiences on registration day. The two students who were not able to come on registration day were pulled into the group by other students and shown the opening procedures. We worked to establish a routine together. We played a get-acquainted game, read and discussed *Peter Rabbit* (Potter 1987), talked about Beatrix Potter books, put together a graph showing how each child would get home at the end of the day, compiled pictures of what each child had discovered that day, and took a discovery walk around the school.

Since six of the students had gone to kindergarten at this school and some of the others had come for an open house the previous spring, the walk was preceded by making a web of what they already knew about the school. After webbing, students walked around the school in pairs, carrying clipboards to copy words or names found written around the school and to record their questions. New discoveries were added to the web after the walk, using a different color. Later in the day, students decided to add a third layer around the web for feelings and questions. We ended the first day by generating a page of significant happenings for the class journal, thus beginning the writing of our class history.

The second day was as busy and filled with discovery as the first. One of the activities was the students' presentations of the picture they had been asked to do in my initial letter to them. The pictures of what they had discovered over the summer looked very different, as a wide variety of materials had been used in their making. As class members asked questions or made comments, they established a context for sharing that lasted throughout the year. Whenever a student presented at authors chair, besides commenting or asking questions about the actual discovery, students always asked about the picture, "What materials did you use?"

This question related back to the students sharing comments during their first presentation to the class.

As we moved through the first few weeks, the rabbit symbol continued to play a role in discovery. A small stuffed rabbit went home each day with a different student. The next day, that student would share a story he or she had written about the rabbit during authors chair. These stories were put into our first class book.

At the beginning of the year, as we began to explore the Discovery concept, we concentrated on many individual and class activities. We started with the familiar, what children wanted to share with each other, and also what they wanted to learn about each other. This focus helped us establish our community of learners. Students shared their ideas and opinions, interviewed and introduced each other to the class, and created "All About Me" books. Reading and writing work time gradually changed from a time of class projects and activities to help students learn classroom procedures to a time for students to explore their own interests and questions. We compiled a list of children's questions, wrote and drew reflections in literature logs and observation logs, and became involved in discoveries about ants and strategies for solving mathematical problems. The focus on ants came from a pilot science project in our school that we related to our exploration of Discovery. After our initial talk and exploration of Beatrix Potter books, we created text sets that promoted wandering and wondering whenever students developed new questions and interests that they wanted to pursue.

Moving to a Focus on Families

After making and presenting books about themselves, students interviewed their parents and took notes about significant events for each year of their own lives. They used this information to put together personal time lines that they presented to each other. This focus on personal time lines led to an exploration of families through oral and written sharing of family stories, histories of their own families, family time lines, and family trees. Students were moving from self and the classroom context into their own families and family histories.

As children talked to their families, took notes, and collected information for their individual time lines, the subject of family trees started

115

appearing in conversations. Several students had seen family trees at home and discussed what they looked like physically. A parent volunteered to come to the classroom and show a family history quilt, a family time line, and a family tree. Students asked many questions during and after her presentation. They decided they wanted to make their own family trees.

Students chose construction paper for the background and for a bare branch tree. After the tree was secured to the construction paper, each student cut out large circles to represent each person living in his or her household. The names were written on the circles and glued to the branches. Some students wrote "mom," "dad," "brother," and so forth instead of names. Some included pets. They also cut out smaller circles and glued them around the outside to represent other family members they knew, but who did not live in the same house with them. (Figure 6.1 shows one student's creation.)

Each student presented his or her tree to the class. The presentations led to a discussion about what makes a family and the discovery that there are varying numbers and combinations of people in a family. Students described a family as anyone who lives in the same house with them. This definition gave children a nonthreatening way to talk about a variety of family structures, including grandparents and great-grandparents who lived in the household, adoption, biracial households, and students who lived in more than one household.

A child who lived with his mother and visited his father on the weekends put his father on the outside of the tree. Another child decided to put two trees on his picture to represent his family at his father's and his family at his mother's. A discussion developed during one presentation because there were few names around the tree. The child had recently been adopted and had not yet met many family members outside of the household. This child was able to connect to another child in the class who had also been adopted. Listening to each other's presentations and looking at the family trees helped children return to a previous discussion of each other and how they are the same and different.

Student Awareness of Cultural Diversity

Students in my class came from many cultures, so cultural awareness played a role in the Discovery focus. After playing a get-acquainted game the first day of school and finding that some students spoke Chinese, Vietnamese, and Spanish at home, one of the earliest inquiry questions was "Why do you speak another language at home?" We started each day

Figure 6.1
Family Tree
(J. T., Age 6)

with a "Good Morning" song in several languages. By the end of the first week we had added Chinese and Vietnamese verses to the song (Spanish was already included).

While we continued to study family history, students also became interested in exploring how they were the same and different. The group's diversity became more evident in discussions when students shared family stories and family trees. Maggie was very aware of her Hopi background; she continued to share Hopi stories and traditions through-out the year. Her dad made a trip to the reservation to get (blue corn) piki bread for us to sample. Erick shared the story of his grandfather and the history of his family, who lived in Peru. He told how he, his parents, and his sister left the rest of the family to come to the United States. Grace and her family shared their Chinese New Year traditions with us, present-ing a lion dance, food, music, and good luck money envelopes. Dominic shared the Vietnamese New Year traditions of his family. This sharing promoted further discussion and comparison of the Year of the Chicken (Chinese) and the Year of the Rooster (Vietnamese) as we looked at New Year's celebrations from different perspectives.

Throughout the year, students continued to share family experiences and traditions. They were interested in what happened in families based on the cultural background of that family. Questions were often heard: How do you do that in your family? Is it hard to switch back and forth from Spanish to English? What is life like on the reservation? They talked about foods, eating utensils, and family traditions. Many discus-sions also developed about adoption, skin color, biracialism, and differ-ences in family religion practices.

Children talked about Jewish holidays when some of their classmates were absent for the holiday, and this prompted a discussion on religion in general. Buddhism was discussed, as well as the difference between being Catholic and Baptist (students wanted to know why both were Christian religions). As students started writing stories and books, the titles reflected their interests. *All About the 9 Jewish Holidays* was presented in authors chair, followed by student books titled *Jewish, Christian, and American Holidays*; *How My Family Celebrates Christmas*; and *All About Our New Year's Celebration*. Discussions led to writing, and students' writing prompted class discussions.

Lilly wrote a series of books about the elderly when her great-grand-mother came to live with the family. (Figure 6.2 shows one of her stories.) Students used family stories as a basis for sharing, reading, and writing. They kept adding to a text set about families, which eventually led to a set specifically about grandparents. Most of these books were later used to explore change over time. They read family stories, shared their family stories, asked many questions of each other, compared family histories, and decided to create a class book of their family history stories to celebrate their diversity.

The students' discovery started with self and each other, but it did not end there. The initial talk about themselves and the classroom grew and expanded. As the school year progressed, they talked about families, culture, history, Christopher Columbus, different biomes, and the people who live in these biomes. During these discussions the questions and Discovery focus were connected back to students, family, and the classroom community. Cultural awareness developed and evolved into an appreciation for cultural diversity (Grant 1977).

Fitting into a Preexisting Curriculum

I had developed a curriculum around countries and world cultures during the previous three years with the support of a parent volunteer who was a children's librarian and a second- and a third-grade teacher at my school. We created country studies within which students could develop their own questions. This project started in first grade with a weekly country presentation by the parent volunteer and developed into a cooperative effort by the students of the first, second, and third grades as they pursued their own questions related to the country studies and shared across grade levels. This process had grown and changed from being completely adult directed to one in which the teachers set up the basic structure and students made choices within that structure.

I wasn't ready to give up this process. I liked the idea of students working across grade levels and presenting their findings to each other. I also liked having a support group of teachers in my school. During the summer I met with this group of teachers at my school for planning-to-plan sessions, and we decided to expand the country studies to compare countries from a common biome. Each class would study a country within a particular biome, such as the rain forest, and then share with each other. I wanted to continue working with this group in my school as well as the teacher research group on discovery. We agreed to continue the cross-grade-level study and to begin the year with the ocean biome as the connector across our classes. We would study Portugal, Spain, and the Caribbean and present to each other.

Figure 6.2
Family Story About Great-Grandmother and Her False Teeth (Lilly, Age 6)

WHEN GRANDMA COMES TO LIVE WITH ME

Written and illustrated by Lilly June Felton

When Grandma comes to live with me I like it. She has false teeth. She plays with them in her mouth.

I have to be careful and not run in the house or I could trip her.

I also need to be quiet when she is sleeping because she might be grumpy if I wake her up.

She also is very fragile because her skin is getting wrinkled, so she has to use a walker.

She has pills and I have to make sure I don't touch them when they fall on the floor. If I eat the pills I might die.

She has to go to the doctor a lot because she is old.

She needs lots of hugs and kisses to make her happy so I give them to her.

By talking about Columbus and his relation to these geographic locations and pursuing the questions that the students developed, I thought I would be able to connect this cross-grade-level study to the Columbus quincentenary and my research with Kathy, Jean, Julie, Gloria, and Kathleen. I knew that we had not given the students any choice in the broad focus of Discovery, the biomes, or countries, but I felt that student inquiry could still develop within this framework. We tentatively planned to expand to country studies within the biomes of rain forests and temperate forests after the Columbus focus ended, giving the students a choice of countries to study. My class would focus on Spain for the first country study, and I would coordinate with both groups to ensure the studies fit together.

What I realize now, which I didn't realize then, was that I was working within a predetermined curriculum that would limit students' inquiries. I thought that because I had managed to make the first country studies fit with the broad concept of Discovery, it would not be difficult to continue to follow the teacher-developed curriculum, with the students pursuing their questions within these topics. As I look back, I realize what I was calling "planning to plan" was really planning. As I reflected during the year, I saw that I had taken the negotiation of curriculum away from students by setting up a structure that limited their inquiry on topics outside the biome studies. Students had real inquiry interests and they also had a lot of easily answered, factual questions that were directly related to the biome/country study rather than to the broader-based Discovery focus. Students asked questions during the Columbus study that were not pursued fully because of the need to stay within the predetermined curriculum of biome studies. As the year went on, I became more aware of students' own questions and I realized that the structure was preventing them from having time to pursue other issues and topics. The interaction between grade levels was valuable, but there needed to be another way to accomplish this interaction. Students' understandings expanded over time. They developed interesting questions and made connections within the biome studies that followed—questions that related back to Columbus, to family history, and to cultural diversity. They had other questions, however, that did not get pursued because of the biome studies.

I still wonder what would have happened if we had not had a predetermined curriculum to follow after the Columbus study. Having each of the three classes study an area significant in Columbus's life was a good beginning because it gave the students a broad context and a starting point. It also opened up all kinds of possibilities for student inquiry that my class did not pursue, except superficially, because I had already determined where we would go next.

During the first few weeks, when we were talking about different perspectives, I read *The Goat in the Rug* (Blood and Link 1976) to the class. There were many questions in the discussion about this story. Some students were interested in how natural materials were used for dyes. Others were interested in comparing how daily life was different at the time of this story than it is in present times. Another group was interested in the role of animals in stories—how some took on human characteristics and some did not. Other students were interested in changing the goat's story and other familiar stories so the stories were told from the perspective of a different character. These were groups of collaborate thinkers, but we had a schedule to follow and so we did not stop to pursue these new interests.

We spent the first few weeks of school establishing the routine, focusing on discovery of self and family, completing the initial interview questions and activities, and talking about perspectives. We continued with family and family history activities, questions, and discussions. We also moved on to talk about Christopher Columbus and Spain.

A Look at Columbus

Because we had made personal and family time lines and had used time lines as a tool in other areas, students were interested in what was happening in Spain before Columbus sailed. They had been reading and browsing books in the classroom, studying the events and the order in which they occurred. One of their reoccurring questions was "How did Columbus get ready for his trip?" The school librarian and I helped the students work through a whole-group research project on this question. After putting together their questions, notes, and webs, and revising and editing, they created the following narrative:

> Columbus had to figure out where to go. Sailors talked about how to get
> to Japan by staying on the 30th degree, so he tried to stay on the 30th

degree by using special instruments. One of the instruments was used to look for the North Star. The instrument looked like a telescope that had a string hanging down. The string told the degrees. They used a sundial during the day to see if they were going the right way.

Another problem was he didn't know what to take on the journey. Columbus predicted what to take on the journey after talking to other sailors. Since other sailors had gone on shorter trips, he estimated how much to take for a longer journey.

The ship was loaded with lots of different kinds of food, including biscuits, beans, water, wine, salted fish, fruits, and vegetables. He brought pigs, horses, and cows in case they needed fresh meat and milk. Once they got to land, the horses could be used for riding.

This narrative was included as a chapter in the book on Columbus and Spain the class decided to write after their research and inquiry. It was also shared when they gave a presentation to the second and third graders. This information stayed with them all year, and some of the seven groups included all, while others included most, of the ideas on their Columbus webs at the end of the school year.

The narrative did not answer some of their original questions about what was happening in Spain before the trip. That information was on their web, but they chose not to put it in the narrative. They became interested in estimating after learning how Columbus estimated how many supplies to take, so we spent time estimating various amounts in all areas of our classroom and homes. Later, students had more discussions about why money wasn't available for the journey. They talked about the king and queen of Spain and compared them to present-day kings and queens. Students wanted to know if Taiwan, Peru, or Vietnam had a king and queen once they found out that present-day Spain did. Students hurried to find answers. This question could have led to looking at present-day forms of government if we hadn't moved on to the biome study with the other classes.

During our study of Spain and Columbus, students created a five-hundred-year time line out of wooden beads that stretched across the classroom. They added information markers to the time line and continued this procedure throughout the year. They watched videos, listened to Spanish music, and turned a Spanish folktale, "The Elegant Rooster"

(Sierra and Kaminski 1976), into a skit. They browsed text sets of Columbus, Spain, and the ocean. They cooked foods of Columbus's time. A person dressed as Columbus came into the classroom to be interviewed. Students brainstormed what they knew and started an ongoing list of what they wanted to know about Columbus, the people of Spain, the ocean, and how people traveled from place to place. Parent volunteers worked daily with individuals and small groups, reading to them, helping them find answers to their questions, and recording their new questions. Small groups worked together to compile drawings and information gathered from different interest areas to share with each other.

After several weeks, students looked at their questions and information to develop what they were going to present to the second and third graders. The presentation they gave was short, but student-directed as to what was to be presented. Students dressed up in Spanish clothes, gave factual information, showed maps, sang a song in Spanish, and presented their Columbus research story. They also presented artifacts, such as flags, a statue of Columbus, and money. The presentations by the second and third graders were much longer and covered information in eight to ten categories. When we evaluated our own and each other's presentations, the students were struck by the format used by the second and third graders. They felt their presentation was too short and didn't contain enough factual information.

As we read Columbus books, there was much discussion about his appearance. One child wanted to know why he looked different in each book; another noticed that in one book he was described as having freckles, but not shown as having freckles in the pictures. The discussion led back to previous discussions of differences in opinions and perspectives. The students also recalled how twenty-seven different stories and names were given to the rabbit that had gone home with each of them earlier in the year.

Students also were interested in Christopher Columbus's journals, as we kept a class journal of significant class events and each student kept a personal journal (Figure 6.3). They decided that Columbus must have kept three journals: a personal one, a public one, and one for the king and queen. This idea stayed with them the whole year and manifested itself in their final reflections as they wrote about the three journals of Columbus and included it on their webs.

Another area of interest that developed was maps. Students got into a discussion about the sea monsters shown on a corner of a map that depicted Columbus's voyage. One child compared sailing into the unknown to facing a sea monster. Some agreed with her, but others were sure there were real sea monsters in Columbus's day. This discussion led into Columbus's knowing that the world was round. At this point we compared flat maps with the globe, looking for differences. We did an experiment with an orange, cutting and flattening the peel. The students compared the differences in the flat map and the globe back to our earlier discussions about perspective.

As we neared the winter break, we worked with the second and third graders on a celebration of learning to share with parents and the school community. Students worked on songs and skits. They displayed artifacts, maps, and their social studies portfolios. The focus was "Old World, New World." Each family brought a food from the old or new world to share at the end of the presentation. We were integrating our focus on families and community into our world studies (Shockley 1993).

From Discovery to Change over Time

The first half of the school year had passed quickly. After reading *Who Came Down That Road* (Lyon 1992), and talking about how things change over time, we went on to read *Window* (Baker 1991) and *The Sandal* (Bradman 1989). As I listened to students discuss these books, I realized that change over time was becoming their focus in relation to Discovery.

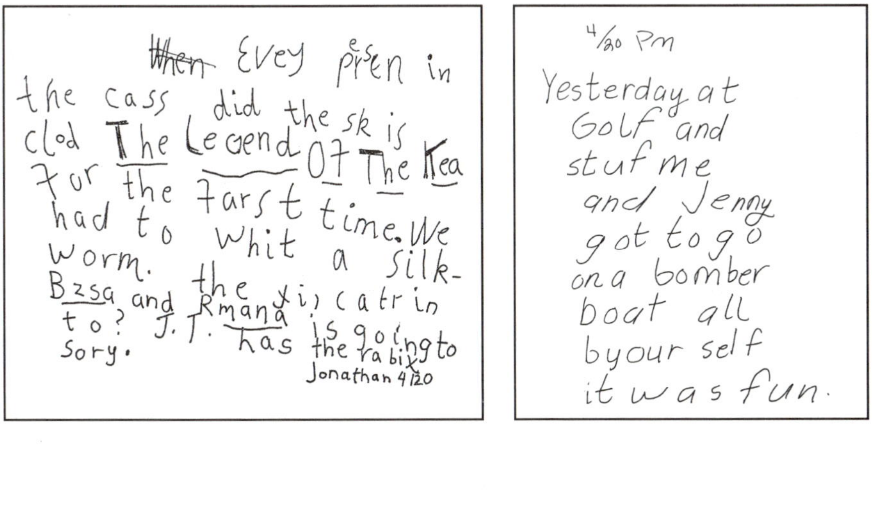

Figure 6.3
*Class Journal
(Jonathan, Age 7)
and Personal Journal
(Tracie, Age 7)
Entries for the Same
Day*

We discussed this idea together, and for the rest of the year students used the concept of change over time as a way to talk about themselves, their families, family histories, Columbus, and the discovery of the Americas. On a personal level, students talked about how they changed over the school year, how their families had changed as they went back and looked at time lines, and how a family does and does not change when they move to a different country, state, city, or neighborhood. Erick was the only student who had moved from another country, so he was bombarded with questions. Change over time also became the focus for science experiments, art projects, and the biome studies. Students were still talking about Discovery, but in relation to how things changed over time.

Students put together a Change over Time text set and continued adding books to it throughout the rest of the year. Our literature discussion groups and literature log entries focused on Change over Time books such as *Crow Boy* (Yashima 1955), *Roses Sing on New Snow* (Yee 1991), and *My Great-Aunt Arizona* (Houston 1992). Someone rediscovered the book *Encounter* (Yolen 1992) in the Columbus text set during silent reading and moved it to the new set. It became the focus for a literature discussion group. This discussion prompted another look at Christopher Columbus books by some students.

During the second half of the year our cross-grade-level studies continued with the focus on rain forests and temperate-forest biomes. Students developed their own directions within these structures and made connections to Discovery and Change over Time. Presenting their findings to the other two classes helped them discover similarities and differences within the biome, and led to new questions. During the rain forest study my class examined Indonesia, while the other classes studied rain forests in Africa and South America. Among other exploratory activities, students tasted Indonesian food and spices, created rain forest layers, studied aerial roots of plants, learned about orangutans, invited a guest speaker to share his slides of Indonesia, tried batik painting, and went on a field trip to the Tucson Botanical Gardens to step into a rain forest. During their presentation to the second and third graders, they had more difficulty deciding what and how to present than they had getting ready for the first presentation. Instead of creating their own topics from their own questions, they decided to use food, clothing, climate, music, and physical location, the same topics the other classes were using.

Research Within the New Zealand Study

During the biome studies, our format was for students to browse the books and artifacts, engage in activities, and listen to speakers before discussing what they knew and listing their questions. They then engaged in research to find answers to their questions. The final biome study of the year was of temperate forests in New Zealand, Germany, and Canada. My class chose to study New Zealand and started by suggesting areas they wanted to pursue such as education, natural resources, people, food, animals and plants, and celebrations. This was a different approach. After they had browsed books and materials on New Zealand, they went back to these categories and developed questions for each area. These questions were more limited to factual information than their previous studies, and I felt they lacked the excitement and interest of the previous inquiry and presentations. Although the students had asked many interesting questions during their wandering and wondering about New Zealand, they ignored these questions and returned to the categories they had listed earlier. These categories had come from the presentations of the second and third graders, and my first graders chose to fit themselves into those same categories without first finding questions that mattered to them and using these to develop their groups. The categories dictated their research and what they presented to the other classes. However, within this research, they did develop another agenda of inquiry.

One of the initiating activities for learning about New Zealand was a guest speaker from New Zealand who now lived in Tucson. During her talk, children became interested in comparing American Indians with the New Zealand native people. Our earlier discussions about the discovery of America and Christopher Columbus had led to questions about how the American Indians were treated. When the students heard that the Maoris and White immigrants lived together with both cultures receiving respect, they wanted more information on American Indians. Maggie was deluged with questions about "her people" that she couldn't answer, so the class decided to pull together a text set to look at the history of the two native cultures. This inquiry existed side by side with the category research students were pursuing to get ready for the presentation to the other grades.

Students were engaged in many activities. Just for fun, we invented a "deep in the woods" song and learned sign language to go with it. We took a legend that explained the different kinds of birds of New Zealand and turned it into a skit to present to parents. Students cooked New Zealand dishes, wove headbands, tried New Zealand games, watched videos of geysers and thermal pools, listened to music, learned some Maori phrases, and chose a sheep as the character to send home each night with a student for writing. Besides these activities, students made maps, created a mural, compared temperate forests to rain forests, examined deciduous tree leaves, explored the location of forest areas in New Zealand, talked about the country's other natural resources, and continued to add to their questions. They also kept going back to consider the two native cultures.

They continued their exploration and comparison of American Indians with New Zealand Maoris. Students read individually according to interest, but "A Hopi Potter" and "Commanche Rider" from *Children of the Earth and Sky* (Krensky 1991) and *The People Shall Continue* (Ortiz 1977) were read aloud for whole-group discussion. The Christopher Columbus, American Indian, and New Zealand text sets were available to students and used by small interest groups. The text sets continued to be the focal point of the study.

We decided to celebrate the end of the biome study by inviting parents to share in our learning. We practiced songs, put together skits, and decided on what artifacts to display. We asked parents to bring in a family recipe and share a food made from that recipe. After the students had completed their part of the presentation, we all stood or sat around the cafeteria sampling the wonderful food, sharing recipes, and talking about their origins. We had presented our skit about New Zealand birds, and the students were colorful birds who seemed to fly as they moved around the room from group to group, sharing in the conversation.

Though the end of the school year was now only two weeks away, the class was not ready to quit. They had learned that Indonesia and New Zealand were both islands. They wished they had chosen the Caribbean instead of Spain for their first study so all of their research would have focused on islands. (I had made the choice of Spain for them and hadn't foreseen this connection.) They wanted to go on and study Australia to see how it compared to the other islands they had studied and how things had changed over time there. There was no other biome study to get in the way of their questions, but the school year was ending and they would be going to another teacher for second grade. However, we did have time for students to engage in short expert projects on a wide range of self-selected topics.

The Ending/Continuation

During the last two weeks of school, the students presented their expert projects and thought together about learning. They evaluated their process of learning and how they had changed. In one discussion, students agreed that small-group discussions were difficult for first graders. They felt that hearing a book or reading it personally did not guarantee that a first grader would have an opinion, connection, or comment to share. As students took charge of their own learning, they had the opportunity to recognize both their strengths and their needs.

Students evaluated the biome and Columbus studies and made suggestions for next year. Ben said, "Webs help me think of what to write, and guest speakers help me get more information. Next year I would like to [again] make a mural." Erick said, "I learned to make a batik because Mrs. Ferguson showed us how, and we saw a batik, and a batik is from Indonesia. I would change nothing next year except I want [to study] the desert." Lilly said, "I would like to learn more about the animals of different countries. I liked it all. Maybe we need to learn more about our oceans around these countries."

A major problem was that the year ended before we were ready for it to end. Students had created a community of learners. They valued and appreciated the diversity within their group. They felt the power of being a group and wanted to take further action as a group, but there was little time left. Students talked about who they were as first graders and what they could contribute to the school. They had been sharing oral and written family history stories all year, working toward publishing a family histories class book. On the next to the last day of school they assembled copies of the book. (Figure 6.4 shows a story from the book.) They were published! They donated a copy of the family histories book to the library. On the last day of school they talked about their classroom community and what they could do for the school the next year. They had contributed their book, but they wanted to do more.

Many students left the classroom crying that day. As students in other classrooms yelled and shouted for joy, they left sad faced or even sobbing. They had worked through a process of inquiry within a community that had really just been getting started.

As I looked back over the year, the questions that students had asked seemed to jump out at me. Why didn't I see those questions and take more time to pursue them? I knew that the next year I did not want a pre-existing curriculum to dictate how much time would be spent on students' questions. I also looked at many of our experiences and realized that they still too closely resembled teacher-directed activities within a thematic unit instead of meaningful firsthand experiences directed by students' inquiries (Bang-Jensen 1995).

Figure 6.4
*Story from Family
History Book
(Joshua, Age 7)*

My Family Tradition
by Joshua

My family tradition for the last 15 years has been to have a reunion. Every two years we have it in Albany, Georgia since 1974. We shared our family secrets. We learned our great grandfather was a slave and how he got our last name.

At our family reunion, they had many different programs the family shared like bowling, talent shows and many family adventures.

I was born in 1986. Then I was able to start going to our family reunion every two years. My family and I travel by car and drive to Georgia. We had a chance to stay in a motel, go swimming, and eat at restaurants.

Family History Stories

I thought about the power of the planning-to-plan idea and of having a support group. I thought about what sort of learning experience the year had been for me. Planning to plan was a beginning, the setting up or foundation for learning. It helped establish the setting and structures in which students could feel comfortable and valued. It was a beginning from which they could go on to pursue their own questions.

With the support of the teacher research group, I was able to reflect, evaluate, ask questions, plan, and look at extensions that I never could have done or even thought about on my own. Sometimes just hearing someone else in the research group talk about the experiences in her classroom helped me understand or look at what was happening in my classroom with a new perspective. I liked having teacher support at my own school, too. I thought about the possibility of teaching with another teacher who was willing to explore a multi-age class. A multi-age class would create the possibility of continuing our inquiry. Having students for a second year would eliminate having to spend so much time at the beginning of every year establishing the routine and creating a community. Students could end the year with ideas for refining the classroom procedures and decide on the questions they wanted to investigate at the beginning of the next school year.

I knew I wanted to be part of a learning community in which questions would not go unexamined. Learning does not suddenly stop when the school year ends. For both students and teacher there are always new questions to explore.

Daily Schedule

8:20	Attendance, morning jobs
	Free reading (students choose books to read)
8:45	Daily opening
	Class secretary calls students to meeting area
	Students lead song, pledge allegiance, moment of silence
	Students present their jobs (contextual math)
9:10	Group meeting
	Math challenge, oral language study, mini-lesson
	Read-aloud
	Students discuss the day's work

9:30   Reading work time
  Read independently or with a group
  Literature circles, shared reading, partner reading
  Readers theatre, poetry, music movement, sign language
  Students may choose to use this as a writing work time

10:35   Outdoor P.E.
  Warm-up lap
  Gross motor activity or game
  Music movement, aerobics, gymnastics (Friday only)

11:10   Writing work time
  Free writing (2–3 days)—writing process on own topics
  Writing invitations (2–3 days)—Pen pals, inquiry writing
  Students may choose to use this as a reading work time

12:00   Lunch and recess

12:45   Personal journal writing

1:00   Class journal and authors chair

1:30   Work time
  Computers, Special Person of the Week, math manipulatives
  and strategy lessons, studies from other mandated curriculum
  topics, options from reading and writing work times

2:15   Chapter book read-aloud (related to inquiry focus)

2:30   Class meeting

2:40   Dismissal

Music, songs, dance, drama, and art are integrated into the work times and are not separate lessons. There are no music, art, or P.E. specialists.

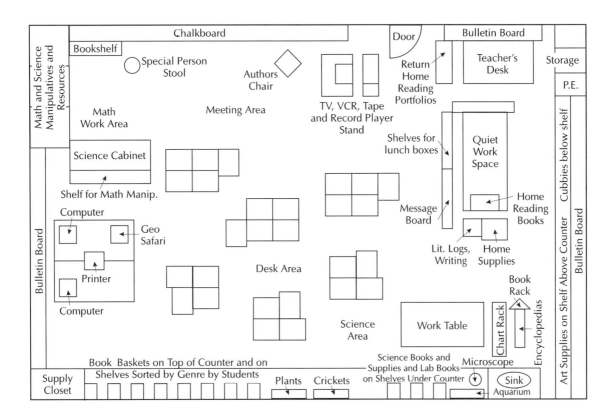

Math and Science Manipulatives and Resources

Chalkboard

Bookshelf

○ Special Person Stool

Authors Chair

Math Work Area

Meeting Area

TV, VCR, Tape and Record Player Stand

Door

Return Home Reading Portfolios

Bulletin Board

Teacher's Desk

Storage

P.E.

Science Cabinet

Shelf for Math Manip.

Shelves for lunch boxes

Quiet Work Space

Computer

Geo Safari

Printer

Computer

Message Board

Home Reading Books

Lit. Logs, Writing

Home Supplies

Bulletin Board

Desk Area

Science Area

Work Table

Book Rack

Cubbies below shelf

Bulletin Board

Chart Rack

Encyclopedias

Art Supplies on Shelf Above Counter

Book Baskets on Top of Counter and on Shelves Sorted by Genre by Students

Supply Closet

Plants

Crickets

Science Books and Supplies and Lab Books on Shelves Under Counter

Microscope

Sink

Aquarium

7 A Long Time Ago When I Was Four: Exploring Inquiry with Young Children

Julie Laird

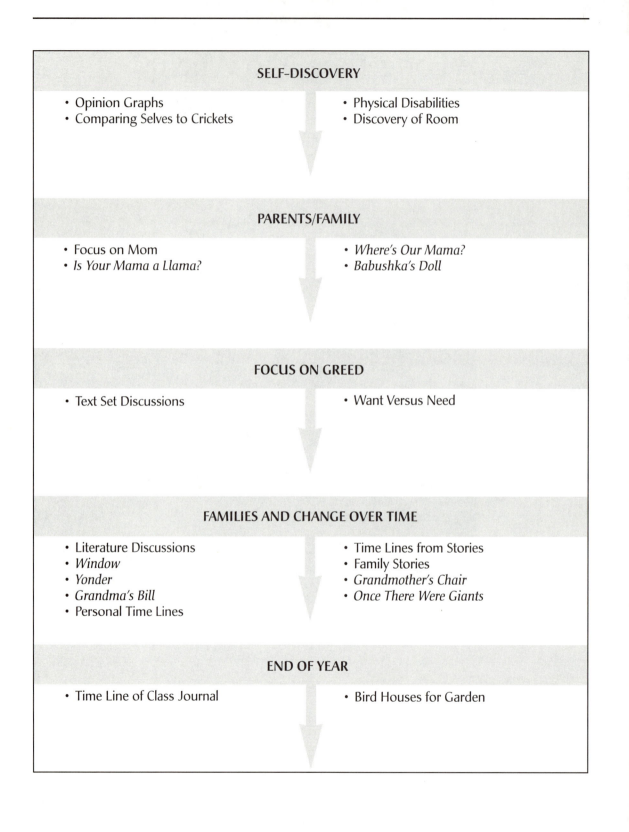

SELF-DISCOVERY

- Opinion Graphs
- Comparing Selves to Crickets
- Physical Disabilities
- Discovery of Room

PARENTS/FAMILY

- Focus on Mom
- *Is Your Mama a Llama?*
- *Where's Our Mama?*
- *Babushka's Doll*

FOCUS ON GREED

- Text Set Discussions
- Want Versus Need

FAMILIES AND CHANGE OVER TIME

- Literature Discussions
- *Window*
- *Yonder*
- *Grandma's Bill*
- Personal Time Lines
- Time Lines from Stories
- Family Stories
- *Grandmother's Chair*
- *Once There Were Giants*

END OF YEAR

- Time Line of Class Journal
- Bird Houses for Garden

"Y OU HAVE TO BE quiet when you want to discover something, so that you don't scare it away." Ian described Discovery after engaging in an initial experience designed to help kindergarten students come to an understanding of this broad concept. Because I anticipated that most would not understand the meaning of the word "discover," I provided experiences that helped them become engaged in the action of discovery. For example, early in the school year, students were invited to wander throughout the room to see what they could discover. As I watched them move around the room, it was difficult to tell what they were focusing on. Periodically, a child would call another child over to look at something specific, but most quietly gazed as they strolled throughout the room.

After about ten minutes, we came together at the rug, and students were asked what they had discovered. Contributions were put on a web that had the word "Discovery" in the middle. We focused on what they had discovered, rather than on the word. As soon as one child said that she had discovered the playhouse, several others chimed in with things they had discovered within the playhouse. They also said they had discovered computers, the writing center, paper, pencils, crayons, cubbies, our library corner, a globe, puzzles, blocks, and many other items around the room. We reviewed this web a couple of times over the following few weeks to see if the children had discovered anything new about the room. We also talked about what Discovery meant to them.

This experience was a way to encourage students to think about Discovery, but it also provided an opportunity for them to become aware of the resources available in our classroom. I hoped that if they were aware of these resources, they would be more likely to ask questions and search for multiple answers to their questions. I also wanted students to begin to have a sense of ownership, and to feel that the things in the room were resources for all of us and that we were all responsible for taking care of what was contained there.

In the remainder of this chapter I describe how the broad concept of Discovery was used throughout the year in a kindergarten classroom with twenty-five students attending a half-day program. I detail some of the experiences that we used to initiate this broad concept, and I give a brief history of the year through the descriptions of these experiences. I also describe how I deviated from the teacher research group's focus, and how later, after listening to students as well as to advice from the research group, I moved the focus back to the students' interest in family and how people and things change over time. Throughout the chapter I explain how kindergarten students can draw from personal experiences in order to gain an understanding of history and perspective. In addition, I explain how the inquiry process occurs differently with kindergartners than it does with older children.

Initiating the Broad Concept of Discovery

In our classroom, we not only explored the environment, but we also took time for students to discover themselves. One way we did this was by drawing self-portraits. Mirrors were placed at each table, and students were encouraged to look at themselves and draw what they saw. For Open House, we hung these portraits on a bulletin board next to an actual photograph of each child. We saved them until the end of the year, at which time students made another self-portrait. I mounted both portraits on a large sheet of paper and included beginning-of-the-year and end-of-the-year photographs. The students enjoyed comparing their drawings, and most commented on their improved artistic abilities.

Another opportunity for self-discovery came about through a series of opinion graphs on favorite colors, animals, toys, and foods. We usually had taste tests before graphing the foods we liked best. Students were consistently encouraged to make their own choices. Through our discussion of these graphs and the process of making them, students explored the concept of perspective. They became aware that people don't always agree, but that it's all right because we are individuals and we are entitled to our own opinions.

As we continued to look at ourselves, I provided a large outline of a person and the students labeled all the body parts they could name. We also discussed and made a chart of everything that we have two of on our bodies. Due to the students' interest in insects, we decided also to look at the bodies of insects. I put several crickets in a dry aquarium, and the students were encouraged to observe them. After a few days, students put single crickets in several baby food jars so that they could observe them more closely. Using magnifying glasses as they observed, we discussed such questions as: How many legs do crickets have? How many body parts? Do they have eyes? How many? Do they have ears? How many?

After the students had observed the crickets for some time, they came to the rug. I wrote "crickets" in the middle of a web and asked them to tell me what they had discovered about crickets. Most students agreed about the number of body parts, but there was one pair of students who insisted that crickets have only five legs. After a brief discussion, another student looked at their cricket and found that, in fact, their cricket did have only five legs. Upon further discussion, the group decided that this cricket must have been injured, and that normally crickets should have six legs.

The next day, I provided an outline of a cricket's body, and we labeled the parts of the cricket that the children had observed. We then took out our human figure for a comparison of the two. We made a chart of the things that were the same and the things that were different on the two bodies.

I had planned to continue comparing other insects, but although the children were fascinated with the insects, their talk kept returning to themselves. I realized that this was where their interest lay; therefore, I needed to allow more time for them to continue to discover themselves.

As we continued to focus on ourselves, I felt this was also a good opportunity to help the students explore their understanding of history and time. I wanted them to be able to make personal time lines from birth to now, but first they needed to understand that events occur in a time order. In order to help students understand this concept, we read many versions of "The Three Little Pigs." I also used this experience to introduce text sets. Each time we read a new version of the story, we discussed it and compared it to those we had already read. We made webs and charts of the comparisons. Students also responded to these stories through art and drama. I then gave them simple pictures from the story and asked them to arrange the events in order on a time line. I was surprised at the number of students who struggled with this task. Some had difficulty with left to right directionality; they weren't sure which end of their paper to start on. Others did not see the relationship of retelling the story with putting the pictures in order. Their pictures were placed in a random order on the time line, even though they were able to retell the story orally in the correct sequence. I realized that we would need more experiences before they could make their own personal time lines.

Moving to a Focus on Greed

Early in November, I decided that we were done exploring self and family and pushed my students into a text set on greed. This was one of the sets our research group had put together during our planning-to-plan sessions before the school year started. Our teacher research group had spent a great deal of time gathering and purchasing books for these sets, and I thought it was time to start using them. When we began the focus, students weren't sure what greed was, but by reading and discussing several stories that had greedy characters, they came to understand the concept.

We discussed *Greedy Gray Octopus* (Buckley 1984), *The Magic Fish* (Littledale 1966), *Four Fat Rats* (Bellows 1987), *The Miser Who Wanted the Sun* (Obrist 1984), *Two Greedy Bears* (Ginsburg 1976), and *How the Grinch Stole Christmas* (Seuss 1957). These books helped the children decide that "someone is greedy if they want too much." They compared the octopus in *Greedy Gray Octopus* to the Cookie Monster from Sesame Street because they saw both characters as having an insatiable hunger. They felt that the wife in *The Magic Fish* was greedy because she should have been happy with the pretty house. During a discussion of this book, students were asked what they would wish for if they found a magic fish. It was interesting to note that even though they had all agreed that the wife was greedy, most still said they would wish for a castle. Many also wished to be king or queen.

Early in December, when children were excited about Christmas, we discussed "needs" versus "wants," and we made a chart comparing the two. There was some contention over whether one "needed" furniture, but students quickly realized how many things they have that they don't really need. I related this to Christmas and other winter holidays and we discussed commercials that try to make children think they need a specific toy. A parent helper was in the room during this discussion, and the next day she thanked me because she said she and her son had continued the conversation at home. He had decided to shorten his list for Santa, saying that he didn't want to be "too greedy."

Throughout our discussions on greed, students made personal connections to the books as well as connections between texts. They even brought books from home that they thought addressed the concept of greed. The problem was that I wasn't sure how the focus on greed related to children's interests and their earlier connections to Discovery. Discussion of this issue with the other members of the research group helped me realize that my students' interests were still on self and family. It made more sense to return to our earlier focus on family, rather than to start another teacher-imposed, preplanned text set. I decided to abandon the greed text set and return to the students' inquiries.

Focus Study on Family and Change over Time

In our focus study on family, we concentrated first on the one member of the family that everyone in the class had in common and talked about frequently: their mothers. I read the book *Is Your Mama a Llama?* (Guarino 1989), we webbed characteristics of the students' moms, and then they drew pictures of their moms. Next I invited students to write or dictate something about their mother. Most chose to describe their mothers, so I read aloud *Where's Our Mama?* (Goode 1991), about two young children trying to describe their mama to a gendarme they have enlisted to help find her. (Figure 7.1 shows one child's description of his mother.)

Later, in order to continue working on the time order of events, I read aloud *Laura Charlotte* (Galbraith 1990), about a stuffed elephant named Charlotte who is passed down through generations; *Grandmother's Chair* (Scott 1990), about a small chair that is passed down through generations; and *Babushka's Doll* (Polacco 1990), about a magical doll that is part of more than one generation. For each of these stories, students dictated the events of the story in the time order in which they occurred. We recorded these events on a long piece of paper, making a time line, and several students illustrated the events. (Figure 7.2 shows the time line we did for *Laura Charlotte*.) Afterward, we talked about how we had made a kind of time line. This experience seemed to help students see the relationship between the order of events and the notion of a time line.

A few days later, I read *Once There Were Giants* (Waddell 1989) and asked whether this story could be placed on a time line. One child responded by saying, "We could, but it would be a long one because it was a long book." I realized that even though they were now able to order events, they were confusing the duration of events in a story with the number of pages and amount of writing in a story.

Figure 7.1
My Mom
(Alan, Age 5)

She likes to shoot guns, wash dishes, and do lots of other things. She has black hair. She's short. She likes to go places.

In order to help them understand the irrelevance of paper length for a time line, I copied the events of our *Grandmother's Chair* time line onto a smaller piece of paper. I showed how two different sizes of paper could contain the same information, and we discussed the issue of size and content.

After these initial engagements with time lines I invited students to make their own personal time lines at home so they could enlist the help of their parents. I suggested they might list at least one important event from each year of their lives, but I encouraged them to use any format that fit their needs. The instructions were open-ended so they could explore and discuss the project with their parents. The variety of completed time lines was absolutely wonderful. (Figure 7.3 shows one of them.) They were all on different colors, shapes, and sizes of paper. Some were centered only on the individual child and included events such as "learned to walk at one year" and "got a tricycle at three years," while others shared family information, such as when a sibling was born. A few were illustrated by photographs of the child at each age. One child had a ten-foot time line that began in 1976, when her parents were married, and included the births of her five brothers and sisters.

The children were very excited to share their time lines with the rest of the class. Almost every child was able to read what was on his or her

Figure 7.2
Time Line of Laura Charlotte

time line. They had taken an active role in making the time lines, even though the majority were written and/or drawn by a parent. We spread the sharing across two days, and when we finished, we talked about where the children had found the information they had included. Their sources included talking to mom, dad, or grandparents and looking through baby books, photo albums, and scrapbooks.

This time line experience was powerful for the children as well as for me because through them we gained an understanding of the children's personal histories. When talking about when something happened, they often explained, "This happened before that," or "This happened when I was a baby." This last comment was most common. Students frequently told stories of silly things they did as babies, such as smearing cake all over themselves or making a mess with something that didn't belong to them. They were intrigued by "baby stories." At one point, I asked them, "When are you no longer a baby?" They weren't able to tell me an age, but they were able to share characteristics that make one "not a baby," such as knowing how to walk and talk, knowing how to drink out of a cup, and not using diapers anymore. Most of their explanations seemed to

Figure 7.3
*Personal Time Line
(Billie, Age 5)*

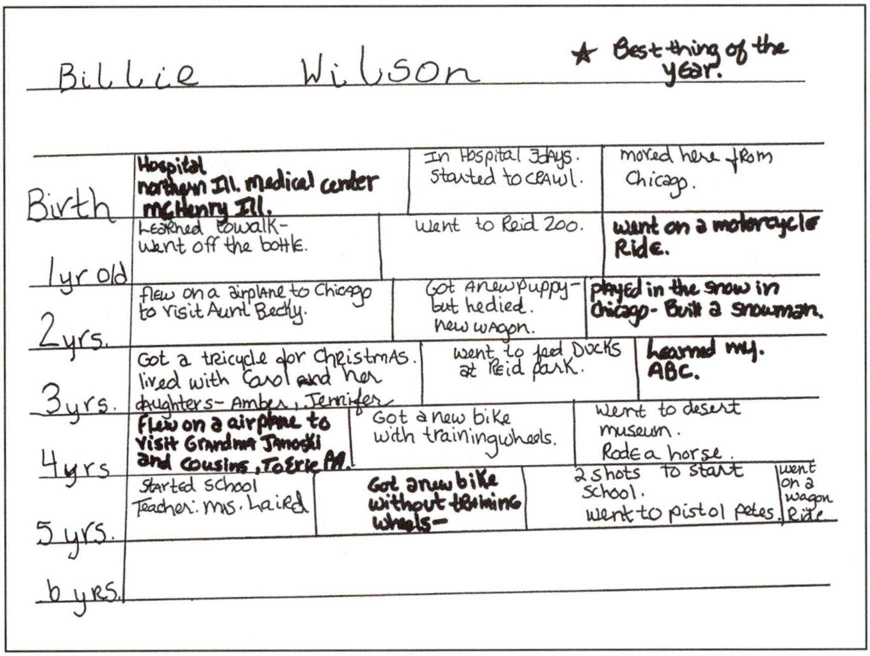

come from experiences with younger siblings; nonetheless, they were aware of these characteristics as strong turning points in their lives, and they were aware that these events were all part of their personal histories.

We returned to *Grandmother's Chair* (Scott 1990) and *Laura Charlotte* (Galbraith 1990). The children were intrigued that the objects that were the focus of these stories (a chair and a stuffed animal) were items that had been part of a family for many years. They began to bring in objects or pictures (drawings or photos) of objects from their homes that their parents had when they were children. As the students shared, their talk continued to foster their understanding of history. Linda described her mother's doll as "fragile" because it was very old. Joshua brought a picture of the day bed he sleeps in that belonged to his great-grandmother many years ago. He explained how his bed was found in a hidden room of his great-grandmother's barn and was believed to have been used for slaves in the Underground Railroad. When students asked Joshua what the Underground Railroad was, he answered, "A long time ago trains must have all been underground, but now they go too far so they had to put them on top of the ground." At this point, I explained what the Underground Railroad really was; however, slavery was an unfamiliar concept to most of the students, and they preferred Joshua's explanation.

As students shared objects from their families, they naturally moved into telling family stories. To encourage their continued inquiry into family history, I asked them to bring in a family story they had dictated to a parent. I asked the children to tell their parents a story, and I asked the parents to write it down in the child's words. I offered suggestions for stories, such as "anything special that happened in your family, such as a family trip, or something special that had happened to the child." I also gave students the option of writing about someone in the family who was special to them. Most of the resulting stories were about family trips. One child wrote about why his dad was special to him. Only one child brought in a story that was not actually about something relating to her family. However, in talking with her, I learned that her dad often told stories at bedtime, and the story she brought was her rendition of one such story. Five students didn't bring a story from home, but they were able to dictate their stories to me in class. Each story was typed; then the students illustrated them and bound them into hardcover books to share with the class and their families. We displayed the students' books in the hall, and parents and other students were encouraged to come and read our family stories.

We continued our focus on family stories until the end of the year, stopping only because summer vacation arrived. We read and discussed many books about families in which changes occurred over time. We had many literature discussions on books such as *Window* (Baker 1991), *When Grandma Came* (Walsh 1992), *Once There Were Giants* (Waddell 1989), *Grandma's Scrapbook* (Nobisso 1990), *Something from Nothing* (Gilman 1994), *This Quiet Lady* (Zolotow 1992), *The Old, Old Man and the Very Little Boy* (Franklin 1992), and *Basket* (Lyon 1990).

For each of these family stories, we engaged in whole-class literature discussions. The students focused mostly on how events and people in the stories changed over time and how the stories all seemed to have a cycle. They were quick to compare the books to one another. They noticed that many of the stories depicted someone starting out as a baby, becoming a child, then an adult, and then having their own child, thus starting the cycle over again. The students were able to note that they had started out as babies themselves, but now they were children, and eventually they would be grown-ups. They all agreed on this, but there was great debate about whether a person had to be married before having a child. Students who thought someone had to be married to have a baby were confused by Crystal's testimony that her mother wasn't married when she recently had a baby. I stayed out of the discussion at this point and became more of a neutral observer. I did let the discussion continue, though, because I felt the students were trying to come to terms with the human life cycle, and the questions they had were valid. When my opinion was sought, I suggested that they discuss the issue with their parents.

The students went on to discuss many other difficult concepts, such as old age, how old one has to be to be old, and death. (They were kind enough to point out that pretty soon I would be "an old lady.") Many students believed that people could only die if they were old, but others acknowledged that sometimes kids die too. They showed a great deal of knowledge about societal problems as they pointed out that people who use drugs or are in gangs often die when they are young.

One book that confused many of the students was *Basket* (Lyon 1990). This is a story about a family who loses a basket during a move to a new home. Everything that they are unable to find is presumed to be in this lost basket. What confused the students was that the illustrations are from many different perspectives. The change in size of the basket in the pictures made them question whether inanimate objects change in size as they get older. Nancy said, "The basket, it was smaller, and then it grew bigger." We looked closely at the pictures to see how size changes when something is seen in the foreground versus the background of a picture. We studied the illustrations more closely and then Crystal said, "It's not getting older, it's just getting old. It's not in age, but it's getting old." Billy helped to clarify: "People that are small grow, but toys don't, but they just get older."

This discussion of age and size continued in the discussion of *Something from Nothing* (Gilman 1994). Students pointed out that people get bigger when they have a birthday, but Fernando challenged this notion when he said, "My Nana Poquita, she's ninety, and she's little."

As we neared the end of the year, our class discussions became more complex. The students had a vast knowledge of related texts as well as personal experiences from which to make connections. They talked about the many changes in their lives. Billy helped to explain: "Each day you do something different, like you go to the store and the next day you probably go somewhere else, or like you learn something new in school. Every day, things just keep changing."

So far in this description of our inquiries, I have focused on our whole-class discussions because it was in these discussions where I felt the class really pushed their thinking with each other. But in addition to the whole-class discussions, we also engaged in short-term small-group work, such as when students formed groups to observe insects. I also set up invitations around the room that involved observing in a nature area, listening to a book on tape, and using writing materials, art materials, and math manipulatives. These invitations were based on the issues and connections that children raised during our whole-class discussions. They were available to children along with the sand and water tables, the block center, the home center, and the outdoor play areas during our work time each day so that they could explore personal inquiries as well as continue to explore questions from our class discussions.

Returning to Students' Interests and Taking Action

Throughout the year, we had an outdoor garden, and students were able to see changes over time through a plant cycle, from seed to harvest. In mid-April, I read *Miss Rumphius* (Cooney 1982). I chose this book because we were nearing Earth Day, and I thought it went along well with this celebration as well as our garden and family stories. After I read the book, we had a discussion about what we might do to make the world a better place. The timing was perfect, because a few days earlier we had had a guest from the Phoenix Zoo. He had brought several animals to share, one of which was a parrot. The students enjoyed the parrot immensely, but when the guest began talking about wild birds, he received lots of groans. I explained that much of our outdoor garden had been eaten by the birds before we had a chance to harvest, and the children were quite irritated. We had tried putting rubber snakes in the garden, but this did not deter the birds. Our guest explained that the birds didn't know it was wrong to eat our garden. He compared it to a child who goes home and eats a plate of cookies, and then gets in trouble for eating them, even though the child didn't know he or she wasn't supposed to. Our guest suggested that we feed the birds so that they would eat the bird seed instead of our garden.

In wanting to take action as Miss Rumphius had, we decided to try out our guest's suggestion to feed the wild birds. I went to the library and collected several books about birds. Back in the classroom, students browsed the books and found a few that had pictures of bird feeders and things birds like to eat. They dictated the supplies they would need, and we sent the list with a note that went home to parents, soliciting their help. It took about a week to gather the materials and food, and then we spent an afternoon making bird feeders and taking them outside to be set up around the garden. The students felt that this was a way to help save their garden from the birds, but it was also a way of doing something nice for the earth, by taking care of the birds. We refilled our feeders periodically until school was out. (I must note, though, that the birds still preferred our garden to the feeders.)

Creating a Class History

As the end of the year neared, we reflected on what we had learned. At the beginning of the year, we had started a log called "Thoughts for the Day." At the end of each day, one student would dictate what we had done that day. The events were written on a small piece of chart paper, and the children read it when we were done. This activity served two purposes: it provided us with a written history of what happened throughout the year; and it was a good review of the day's events so that when the students went home and their parents asked, "What did you do in school today?" they would be more likely to remember. Each day's thoughts were compiled into a book that represented our class history. Periodically, students would sit with this book and read and reflect on their previous experiences.

At the end of the year, we spent several sessions going through this log and using the information it contained to make a time line of the important events that had taken place throughout the year. The students debated as to what should or should not be included on the time line, and they came to the consensus that only "special and important" events should be included. Going to the library or going out to recess was rejected because those things happened regularly. Some of the special things that were included were the carving of pumpkins, the creation of the bird feeders, favorite centers, guests in the class, field trips, and special read-aloud stories that had become class favorites.

Reflection

The summer after the school year described in this chapter, each member of our research group took the time to write a history of the year. I wrote everything I could remember that had happened during the school year. Throughout the year, each of us in the teacher research group had kept a journal, and periodically we made lists for one another of events that had taken place in our classrooms. I used all the data I collected to write the history, but I neglected personal reflection until now. Perhaps that is because reflection is the most difficult part. In rereading my journal entries, I was struck by how frequently I was frustrated with my own lack of direction. We had began this study, as a research group, by looking at the issues of Columbus. However, when interviewing my students during the fall interview, not a single student had ever heard of Christopher Columbus. Of course they were willing to speculate that he was Natasha's cousin or a basketball player, but since none had ever heard of him, I couldn't figure out how I was ever going to be able to help my students begin an inquiry project around Columbus. Instead, I moved aimlessly into the "greed" text set, thinking, perhaps, that somehow this might lead me to Columbus. One entry in my personal journal, dated December 15, says, "I still haven't mentioned Christopher Columbus and the Quincentenary is long over. I wonder if I'll ever get around to mentioning him." Throughout my journal, there are numerous other entries that begin, "I feel frustrated."

When the research group met, I heard the others talk about how their students had decided on topics for inquiry and then had broken into groups to work together and/or independently on their personal inquiries. They talked of students getting information through research at the library, letter writing, guest speakers, and interviews. The other group members' classrooms all seemed to be productive, and I began to feel inadequate because I felt my students were not coming up with topics for inquiry, and they definitely were not forming small groups to work independently. I had no idea how I could reach this point with kindergartners.

Part of the problem I was facing was that I viewed the inquiry cycle too narrowly. I thought that unless my students came up with good questions and formed small groups to research these questions, then I wasn't doing inquiry. That wasn't the case. My students were going through the inquiry process, but I just didn't realize it. Kindergartners have many different interests at the same time, and their interests change frequently. If they ask a question or wonder about something and don't receive a prompt response to their question, they frequently pursue a new focus. Their interest can be rekindled if the preceding topic comes up again. If it doesn't, they often move on to something new. With my students, the issues that kept surfacing were related to the human life cycle and how individuals and families change over time. Even though they continued to participate in other small focus studies, life cycle and family issues seemed to be at the center of all their discussions.

I now realize that this was our inquiry. One of the main differences in our process, compared to the other classes I was hearing about, was that most of our inquiry seemed to occur in a large-group setting. In the past I had used small groups for literature discussions, but this year we met mostly as a whole group for such discussions. Students would sit on the floor in a circle so that they were able to see one another. I frequently compared these discussions to talks that one might have around a dinner table. Students did not raise their hands to talk, but I did ask that they listen to one another and wait until they weren't interrupting someone before they began to talk.

I also realized that much of the inquiry of young children occurs through their play (Rowe 1993). I valued play from a developmental perspective, but I did not originally see it as inquiry. While older children form groups and use a variety of references to investigate their questions systematically, young children "play" their way into understanding. They need a learning environment that contains many materials and resources, adults to answer their questions or read books they request, and sustained time for play. Because I had moved away from one- to two-week thematic units and took long periods of time to explore children's interests in families and change, they had the time they needed to play and think about these issues in greater depth. They could ask new questions and return to previous ones because I had not moved on to the next unit and put away the materials and books that they needed.

When I looked back over the year, I saw that their play at the various areas in the classroom often focused around our class inquiry on change over time as well as their personal inquiries. In the block center, children built homes for families to live in. They also painted large boxes and created homes and communities. They wrote books about and painted pictures of their families. They compared the number and types of people in their families and took on the roles of various family members. Although some of their play involved outdoor experiences, I am now giving greater emphasis to outdoor play in my curriculum.

When given the opportunity to study a topic of interest, such as themselves or their family, students in my kindergarten class were able to make a variety of connections. Their own lives gave them a reference point from which to associate other events in history. It was difficult for them to understand a historical event that happened many years before their birth, but they had learned about historical tools such as family stories, scrapbooks, and photo albums. They also used events in their own lives as historical markers, which helped them put other events into perspective.

The students had many opportunities to be involved in the process of inquiry and gained a strong understanding of history and perspective. Their historical understandings have come mostly from our discussions of families and family cycles. They are aware of similarities and differences between people, and this perspective is one that I believe will continue to develop as they grow older and have more experiences with literature, school, and life.

Daily Schedule

11:45	Opening
	Attendance, pledge, moment of silence, headline news
12:00	Group activities
	Literature circles
	Language arts and math strategies
12:40	Outdoor play
12:55	Shared reading/read-aloud
1:15	Indoor center invitations and play areas
	Invitations using writing, math, and art materials
	Nature observation center
	Listening center (book and tape)
	Math exploration center
	Block center
	Home center
	Water and sand tables
	Construction center
	Classroom library
	Art center
1:55	Thoughts for the day
2:10	Dismissal

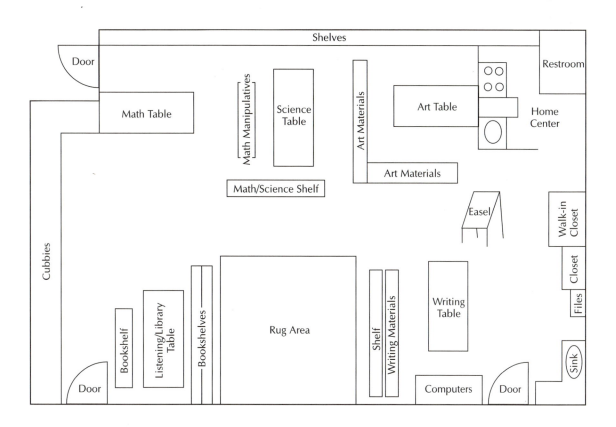

8 What Does It Look Like?
Curricular Engagements Within a Cycle of Inquiry

A S WE WORKED with students and reflected on inquiry, we became increasingly convinced of the necessity for a framework that would support us in putting our beliefs into action (Short and Burke 1991). We had thought about our beliefs and collected possible curricular engagements, but we also needed a curricular framework that would allow us to see the relationships and connections across these engagements. In a textbook curriculum, the framework is linear and based around hierarchical sets of facts in scope and sequence charts. When we moved to thematic units, we fluctuated between choosing activities within that same linear framework and a "grab-bag" framework, where activities were chosen at random from a collection of ideas. Neither of these frameworks was based in our theoretical understandings about inquiry and curriculum.

Because of our earlier experiences with the authoring cycle as a curricular frame for reading and writing (Short and Burke 1991), we knew that this framework was based on the learning process and would support us in planning to plan and in negotiating curriculum with students. For us, authoring was a metaphor for learning, the creation of meaning. Over time, the authoring cycle as a curricular framework for inquiry played an increasingly important role in our thinking about curriculum. We introduced the cycle to children and displayed it on the classroom wall and in course syllabi so that students could use the cycle to think about their personal and class inquiries.

Because this framework is integral to how we think as teachers, this chapter describes the cycle and the kinds of curricular engagements that might be included at each part of the cycle. Figure 8.1 presents our model of the inquiry cycle, as based on the authoring cycle. Though this cycle was introduced in Chapter 1 (see Figure 1.3), in this chapter we explain in greater detail its various components.

In presenting the cycle, we have several qualifications. One is that the cycle is recursive in nature: students continuously move back and forth and across it. The cycle is actually a spiral of experiences that build on one another rather than circle back to start again at the same point (Dewey 1938; Taba 1962). Also, although we list particular engagements for each part of the cycle, many of these engagements can support other aspects of the cycle. We include an engagement at one or two points in the cycle where we feel it is most significant, and have highlighted them by setting them in italics so they can be easily spotted in the text. We have included only a brief description of each engagement. More complete descriptions of the engagements and the cycle itself can be found in *Creating Classrooms for Authors and Inquirers* (Short and Harste, with Burke 1996). Some of the engagements were also described more fully in previous chapters of this book.

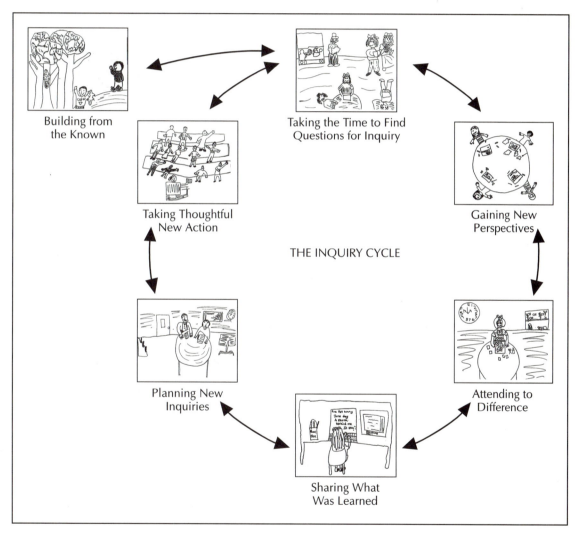

Figure 8.1
The Authoring Cycle as a Curricular Framework for Inquiry

The inquiry cycle is set in motion as the class, a small group, or an individual student moves into a focused study on a particular topic or theme. Deciding on these topics involves a negotiation between the school curriculum, the teacher's interests and experiences, and the students' interests and experiences. Sometimes students initiate a focused study, such as when Julie's kindergarten students kept raising their issues and connections about families and change over time despite her efforts to move them into another focus. Sometimes the focused study is initiated by the teacher in response to students' needs. Gloria began the year with a study of conflict and peace because of difficulties her fifth-grade students were experiencing in their personal relationships both within and outside of school. Even when the focus is mandated by the school, as it was for Kathleen, who had to teach Arizona history in fourth grade, there is still room for negotiation with students. Because her students were interested in culture, she initiated this focus through primary sources and literature about the diverse cultural groups in Arizona.

When the curriculum is organized around a class focus, the most important consideration is that this focus be established through negotiation with students. Within the focus there should be plenty of room for students to find and explore their own inquiries from many different perspectives. The topic may be a class focus, but the problem-posing and inquiry questions should be determined by students. The inquiry cycle may also be set in motion when students engage in individual expert projects that grow out of a personal interest not connected to a particular class focus, but that the student finds personally significant.

Building from the Known

Because we believe that connecting to and building from our life experiences are essential to learning, we plan initial experiences that support

students in making connections to what they already know. Their first engagements need to be open-ended so they can respond with the connections that are most important to them. We used to begin thematic units by teaching students the "background information" we thought they needed. Now we plan engagements that will allow students to explore and make their own connections. Time for students to share their connections and hear each other's voices is absolutely essential. The role of the teacher is to listen in order to get a sense of children's connections and voices.

Conversation, stories, and personal connections are shared as children participate in read-alouds, browse books, listen to music, observe in a nature center, or conduct surveys of family members or classmates. We choose *read-alouds* and have class discussions on books that are close to their own experiences or are old favorites. We set up large blocks of time for *browsing* books, materials, and artifacts and then gather each day for *class sharing times*. We encourage children to tell *stories* through oral sharing as well as through *written reflections*, *free writes*, *sketches*, or by using paint, chalk, and other art materials. Having brief *literature circles* with partners or a small group on a picture book, a short story, or paired books (two books that are related to each other) also supports student talk and sharing.

Engagements that involve students' bringing artifacts, collecting data or stories from their home settings, and talking with each other about their lives are particularly productive in encouraging their connections and stories. One engagement we frequently use is *Getting to Know You* (Short and Harste, with Burke 1996), where students form partners, interview each other, take notes, and write or dictate an article for a class newspaper. At the beginning of the year, these interviews relate to general interests, but later interviews can relate to the class focus. *Family stories* (Short and Harste, with Burke 1996), the "remember when" stories that families often tell at family reunions, offer an opportunity for students to interview family members, take notes, and then share these stories orally or in writing in the classroom. *Interviews* of family members, friends, or neighbors on issues related to the class focus encourage students to bring their experiences outside of school into the classroom. *Time lines* are another engagement that involves interviewing and connecting to life experiences. We have had children construct time lines on important events in their lives, their family history, the changes in their lives, and places they have lived or visited. (Figure 8.2 shows an example.) *"All About Me" books* are places where children write and draw about their interests, family members, home, neighborhood, and so forth. These books build community and self-esteem as well as serve as references for later work in the classroom.

We also encourage children to bring in *artifacts* related to the class focus or broad concept because we find that these artifacts encourage them to reflect on their own connections and facilitate the telling of their stories to classmates. We have asked students to bring an object that reflects something they discovered over the summer, a change they have made, who they are as learners, a structure that is important to them, the community to which they belong, or their sense of place. Often we begin with one artifact and then ask students to bring in a collection of artifacts. Children share their collections with small groups and then arrange them in a *museum* and write labels for their displays. Often the activity *Save the Last Word for Me* (Short and Harste, with Burke 1996) is used to share an artifact or museum display. In this engagement, other students view the artifact or display and talk about what it tells them about that individual. The individual listens, but is not allowed to talk until the others have finished; then he or she gets the last word.

Another related engagement is to ask students to do an *archaeological dig* of some kind. For example, Kathy has asked teachers to dig through their wallets and purses for evidence of their literacy or their sense of

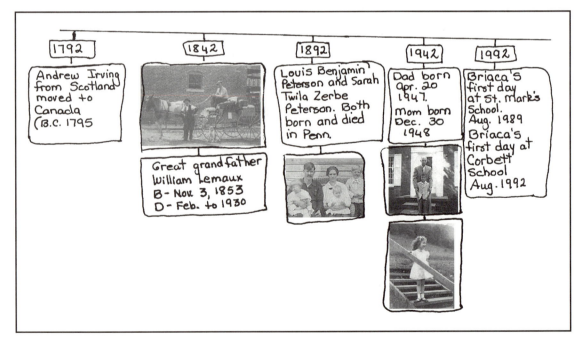

Figure 8.2
Family Time Line (Briaca, Age 6)

place. We've also asked students to look through their backpacks and to examine the contents for evidence of who they are as learners.

These engagements highlight personal and social knowing as the heart of inquiry. Through all of this sharing, students become aware of their own connections and understandings, as do teachers. We listen carefully and take notes on class charts or ask the students to record these connections in their journals. Sometimes we plan webbing, brainstorming, and discussion engagements that are designed for us to discern children's current understandings, such as those we used for the *small-group interviews* during the Discovery focus (see Chapter 2). Students' own experiences become the base from which further exploration of the topic occurs. As they continue their exploration, students are pushed to extend their learning into new areas and gradually develop specific questions to pursue.

Taking the Time to Find Questions for Inquiry

Eve Merriam helped us understand why inquirers need to slow down and take the time to explore. In *The Wise Woman and Her Secret* (1991), a group of villagers arrive at an old woman's house demanding the secret of her wisdom. When she refuses, they search everywhere but finally return to their village. Jenny, a young girl, lags behind as she explores cobwebs, twigs, and a penny that is green from years at the bottom of a well. Full of questions, she shows the penny to the old woman, who tells Jenny that she has found the secret to wisdom. Jenny looks at her in surprise and asks what the secret is. The old woman replies that it is taking the time to look,  listen, smell, and observe the world around her; to "wander and wonder" about the world.

This part of the cycle highlights the role of "wandering and wondering" in inquiry (Short 1993). Students are given time to wander and explore a topic from different perspectives and to wonder about many aspects of life. They do not have to immediately develop a question for investigation, but can take time to explore new understandings, collect interesting facts and ideas, and notice contradictions and connections in their learning.

Barry Lopez (1992), a naturalist, argues that to learn something about nature, we are obligated to "pay attention rather than constantly pose questions"; to listen and really "be *in* a place" before we have the right to ask questions (p. 36). Through observation, an interest or feeling of tension begins to grow, and this gradually leads to a focused question.

We used to begin a focused study by urging students to quickly find a topic or question to research. We immediately had students brainstorm what they knew and what they wanted to know. We concentrated on the research itself and not on how students went about finding and posing their questions. The problem was that the resulting questions often were the superficial "How big is Mars?" variety, which could be answered quickly. Many times they didn't even ask a question but simply gathered information on a topic, such as spiders or rockets. They collected facts on their topic without any real sense of need or desire to know. They did not consider these facts within broader issues but gathered interesting, but isolated, facts to put in a report and "cover" the topic. Often they didn't even ask their own questions. We would provide a list of topics or questions, and students would choose one for a group.

Although we have spent a great deal of time as educators developing research strategies, we have not thought much about how to support the search for questions in the first place. As we explore wandering and wondering with our students, we have begun to get a sense of the structures and engagements that support students as they "muck around" in a topic, but we still have much to understand. We aren't used to encouraging students to explore in order to find significant questions. We believe that wandering and wondering must include examining a topic as broadly as possible from many different perspectives and through conversation and observation. These experiences push students to go beyond what they already know and to develop broader understandings from which their own inquiries can then develop.

Many of the engagements we use in this phase of the cycle are similar to those that were part of the "building from the known" phase, except that the focus here is on bringing in a wider range of perspectives on the topic. In fact, these two aspects of the cycle flow continuously back and forth and are often difficult to distinguish from each other. As students listen to others share their stories, connections, and artifacts, they have already begun to consider new perspectives and understandings. We continue to *read aloud* to students, but we choose books that go beyond the connections and experiences that children have already shared. We add a greater diversity of books, materials, and artifacts to the classroom for *browsing*. In gathering resources for browsing, we look for texts from different sign systems related to the focus—books, pieces of music, art prints, cultural artifacts, dance videos, and so forth. We also search for materials that reflect the perspectives of different knowledge systems—for example, informational books from a scientific perspective, historical fiction from a historian's perspective, brochures from a farmer's perspective, maps from a cartographer's or traveler's perspective.

Often these resources are organized into *exploration centers* that are set up around the room. Most of these centers do not contain activities per se, but consist of a related set of materials in a small basket or tub for students to explore. Students explore the materials at these centers and informally record their observations and wonderings through writing and sketching. Usually a particular time period is designated for the exploration centers and is followed by a *class sharing time*. Instead of leading the class step by step through a series of activities we have planned to teach a particular topic, we empty our files and put out all of the materials in centers for them to explore so they can consider many dimensions of the topic. Some engagements still involve the whole class, but most are put in the exploration centers.

Whole-class engagements might involve exploratory *field studies*, such as observing birds at a feeding station, noting nearby traffic patterns, planting a garden, sitting in the desert, or sketching the layout of their bedrooms. The focus is on close observation and then sharing these observations through conversations. Students support their observations by sketching and informally recording them.

As in the building from the known phase, lots of time for talk and sharing through *class meetings* is essential so that students have many conversations about their observations. While much of this talk occurs in frequent, short class meetings, other times students share in small groups. Students bring their jottings and sketches in *journals* to facilitate their sharing. In their small-group and class meetings, they often use *webs* and *graffiti boards* to capture their in-process ideas and questions. On a graffiti board, each person in the small group takes one corner of a large sheet of paper and jots down words, phrases, ideas, and images as they engage in various explorations. Students then share with each other from their individual graffiti. Webs can capture and organize whole- or small-group brainstorming about topics and issues. While informal sketching and writing tend to be the primary sign systems used to record their explorations, students also use *graphs*, *charts*, and *diagrams* to record their observations and engage in *improvisational drama* on issues or events they are trying to understand or explore.

As particular areas of interest emerge from class meetings and student journals, *text sets* (Short 1992) can be put together. These sets support students in closely examining certain subjects to determine whether there are questions they want to pursue in greater depth. Sometimes the text sets become part of the browsing, as they were during the Discovery focus. Other times the text sets are used in *literature circles* (Short and Pierce 1990). Children sign up to read and discuss one text set in a small group of four or five students over a week or two. Literature circles of *shared book sets*, multiple copies of a picture book or chapter book, can also be organized so students can look at an issue more closely to find questions for inquiry. These discussions are often supported by *webs*, *graffiti boards*, *Save the Last Word for Me* (using quotes from the books), *Anomalies* (lists of what puzzles them as they read), *Sketch to Stretch* (a sketch of the meaning of the story to them), or *comparison charts* (Short and Harste, with Burke 1996). (Figure 8.3 shows a sample comparison chart.)

Literature circles encourage students to look more closely at an area of interest or tension and to consider the perspectives of others through books and dialogue. They can provide a bridge between exploration centers and focused inquiry by helping students find the in-depth questions they want to pursue.

Another engagement that encourages students to talk and consider others' perspectives is *Say Something* (Short and Harste, with Burke 1996). In pairs, two students share the reading of a picture book or short story. One student reads aloud a chunk of text and then stops, and both students say something (a comment, question, prediction, or connection). The second student then reads the next chunk of text, and both again say something.

Throughout this wandering and wondering, it is essential that students keep track of the questions and issues that naturally develop from their ongoing engagements and conversations. With young children, large *class inquiry charts* seem to be most effective. As questions, issues, or "I wonder" statements come up in discussions, they are recorded on these charts. Comments that reflect students' current understandings and connections can also be recorded on class or small-group brainstorming webs. Students can also record their questions through free writes, sketches, and lists in individual *learning logs*, in special *"I Wonder"* booklets,

The Gold Coin And A Day's work

Same	Different
– both Poor	– one stealed and one didn't
– both lied a lot	– one liked The L.A. Lakers and one didn't
– They both Needed Money	– one Traveled a Lot, one din't
– They both Cared	– one had a boy helping and one didn't
– They both worked in Gardens	– one was a Thief and one wasn't
– They each had littel houses.	
– They both Tried to be another Person	

The book Made a difference by . . . .

• They each helped	• They didn't They worked For There own share.
• They each worked to Get money instead of Stealing + lying.	• They lied and They made up For it.
• They Were Poor + They Made The best of it.	• They cared For each other.

Figure 8.3
Comparison Chart of Paired Books (Christina and Sadie, Age 10)

or in a list kept in student work folders. The essential point is that their questions be recorded on an ongoing basis; if they are not, they may be forgotten or overlooked as students select a focus for in-depth inquiries.

To facilitate the move to in-depth inquiries, students often return to their charts or lists of questions as a class and mark with a star the ones they consider significant. These significant questions or issues are then categorized to make groups of related questions, which become the basis for small-group, individual, or class inquiries. Older students can return to the charts, journals, and exploration centers to record the topics, issues, and questions that they are most interested in pursuing on separate slips of paper. They then meet in small groups, combine their ideas, and move the slips of paper around to create categories. The small-group categories and lists are then combined to create a whole-class web of possible inquiries.

Through this process of observation, conversation, and selection, students develop questions for inquiry that go beyond facts to broader conceptual issues. During their explorations, students enjoy learning new facts about the topic, but these facts then become part of their inquiry into bigger questions instead of the focus of their research. Through this process of finding questions that are significant to them, students then engage in focused inquiry.

Gaining New Perspectives

As students move into focused inquiry, it is essential that they examine their questions from new perspectives to increase the complexity and depth of their research. We encourage them to explore different

perspectives through collaboration, investigation, and transmediation. Because we believe that it is through collaboration that students consider other perspectives and go beyond their current understandings, we encourage students to form groups where they actually think with others, not just cooperate to complete a task. Collaboration prompts them to consider new ideas and explain their thinking to others. Students can also gain new perspectives on their inquiries through transmediating across different sign systems (Siegel 1995) and investigating across the perspectives of different knowledge systems (Harste 1992). The learning environments that support focused inquiry therefore need to facilitate collaboration and include many different resources, materials, and tools from a range of sign systems and knowledge systems related to students' questions.

The most typical organizational structure for focused inquiry is to form the class into groups of four or five students. These *inquiry groups* are developed from categories of the students' questions and concerns. Students select the group that most interests them. Sometimes, student questions are too diverse. In this case, students engage in *individual* or *partner inquiries*. Other times, one central issue emerges. In this case, the class can explore this issue through whole-group discussions and engagements as well as *experience centers* (Burke 1992), where they explore the topic through some kind of investigation. Experience centers differ from exploration centers in that students use experience centers not just to browse through the materials but also to investigate through observation, experimentation, reading, and so forth. Here students find open-ended engagements that encourage them to consider other perspectives or use new tools, research methods, or materials in their inquiries. Experience centers provide invitations to new ideas that students can choose to explore during work times. They work especially well with young children as a way for them to extend their inquiry rather than meeting in small groups.

Once questions for inquiry have been selected, an *inquiry plan* is developed. The class, group, or individual lists the question or questions, what needs to be done to examine those questions more closely, and the materials needed for the inquiry. Teachers and students share responsibility for gathering these materials. The inquiry can take the form of a *literature circle*, where students read and discuss a shared book or text set, or *field studies*, where students gather their research in settings outside the classroom. In other cases, students may gather a wide range of *resources*, including literature (fiction, poetry, and informational books), pieces of music, art prints, videos of dances or dramas; *outside experts*; and/or *primary sources* (diaries, artifacts, and so forth). Students can be encouraged to take a variety of perspectives based on different knowledge systems by including books and materials that reflect these different perspectives in their sets of resources or inviting outside experts into the classroom who have different backgrounds. Another strategy is to ask students to consider their topic from the perspective of a certain role or profession— farmer, banker, teacher, child, parent, archaeologist, environmentalist, and so forth—and to list questions and research tools from each of these perspectives.

Transmediation, the movement across different sign systems, also encourages students to consider new perspectives. *Sketch to Stretch* involves students by encouraging them to take their understandings from one sign system (language, in this case a book) into another sign system (art). In making this connection across sign systems, students cannot simply transfer meaning from one system to the next because of different meaning potentials in these systems. Instead they must transform their understandings and consider new meanings and perspectives (Siegel 1995). (Figure 8.4 presents an example of a Sketch to Stretch activity.) We have also used *reflective drama*, where students take on the roles of characters from their research or from literature (O'Neill 1982; Edmiston 1993). In reflective drama, students may work in pairs, with one person a reporter who interviews the other person, who takes on the role of a character. Or they may create a tableau, where the members of a small group arrange themselves in a still life that embodies a significant scene from

Figure 8.4
Sketch to Stretch: Response to Less Than Half, More Than Whole *(Lacapa and Lacapa 1994). "We fought all the time in third grade, and now we are learning to get along with each other and respect each other like the boys in the book. These represent our two hands reaching out to each other" (Brooke, Age 11, and Thea, Age 10)*

their research or reading. Or they may create an event that is not a re-creation of a scene from a book but an extension of their research and reading. Reflective drama is not a performance for others but a way for students to push their thinking about people and events they encounter in their investigations.

As students investigate, they read, engage in observational field studies, develop experiments, conduct surveys, interview experts, write letters to get information, and examine artifacts and other primary sources. Young children often use *book-and-toy sets* (Rowe 1993), text sets that combine books and toys. Instead of separating the book center from the toys, books about machines, for example, are put with the trucks and bull-dozers, and books about zoo animals are put with the animal collections. These sets are often organized in boxes or crates set up around the room so that children are encouraged to integrate their play with books.

In their investigations, students use many different tools for collecting and organizing their ideas and data. These tools also allow them to observe and reflect on their ideas. While *written notes* are important, students need to have many other tools available to them; and it is easy to overrely on journals. They also need mathematical and visual tools, such as *graphs, comparison charts, maps, Venn diagrams, flow charts, webs, time lines*, and other diagrams. They need to sketch as they observe closely and to dramatize as they try to think through motivations or particular events. In addition, young children use imaginative outdoor and indoor play as an important inquiry tool.

To support students in their inquiries, particularly when students are engaged in small group or individual inquiries, the teacher will probably need to offer *strategy lessons* (Goodman and Burke 1980) on specific inquiry strategies such as interviewing, using time lines, writing letters, notetaking, creating surveys, constructing graphs, and reading informational materials. As students engage in their investigations, the teacher should also plan whole-group engagements that will support the small-group or individual inquiries. Sometimes these involve demonstrations or lessons to provide important information that students are requesting, or discussions and experiences to introduce other perspectives for them to consider.

Sometimes as the class brainstorms a web of possible topics for inquiry and students choose the ones they want to explore, there are more areas on the web than there are groups. If so, the class can choose one of these areas to explore as a whole class while the others are being investigated by small groups or individuals. This *whole-class inquiry* can demonstrate the ways in which students might go about their own inquiries as well as create a conceptual context for their small-group inquiries.

Another important role of the teacher is the careful selection of *read-aloud books*, particularly chapter books. Read-alouds should introduce new perspectives and encourage conversations about larger conceptual issues. The discussions of the read-aloud can provide an important context within which students pursue their own inquiries more thoughtfully and critically and make connections with a broader range of issues and perspectives.

While gaining new perspectives highlights students involved in their own inquiries on questions that are significant to them, teachers play an important role in providing a learning context that both supports students in their investigations and challenges them to consider other possibilities and connections. This context includes time for students to reflect on their investigations without pressure to produce a product too quickly.

Attending to Difference

Children are constantly faced with perspectives and ideas that challenge their thinking as they interact with others. They come to understand their

own perspectives through having to explain their thinking and to consider new perspectives through listening to the ideas of others. They also encounter other perspectives through reading literature, interviewing informants, and exploring a wide range of primary sources. They feel tension as their understandings and ideas are challenged, and they need quiet, reflective time to reconsider what they believe and understand related to their inquiry.

Because time spent in the inquiry groups is often a time of intense dialogue where many ideas and issues are raised, students need a quiet place away from their group where they can think and consider those ideas. Having time to sketch or write in their *inquiry journals, reflection logs,* or *learning logs* becomes an integral part of the inquiry process because it is during these quiet reflections that students are able to make the ideas their own. *Group meetings* and *class logs* facilitate reflection, but it is important that students also have an opportunity periodically to reflect as individuals. These reflections support them in pulling together their ideas into some kind of unity to share with others through presentations.

Sharing What Was Learned

At some point, learners need to go public with what they currently know and understand about their inquiry focus. While inquiry is a never-ending process, students create understandings through their investigations that satisfy their immediate desire to explore their original question and they are ready to examine other topics and questions. Through presentations, they pull their ideas together to present formally, but not finally, to others. The process of pulling together their understandings allows students to figure out what they currently know and ask new questions. Through presenting, they transform what they and others know.

When the class moves into presentations, some students may feel they are still in the middle of their inquiries while others are at a point of closure. Presentations are appropriate for both because they support students in pulling together what they know at that point in time. Presentations do not assume finality—that the research must be complete and finished; they simply provide an opportunity for students to determine what they have learned and are ready to share with others at that point in time.

Students present their research using a wide range of sign systems. They do not just automatically write informational reports. Sometimes research is presented through *informal sharing*, where the groups or individuals briefly share their process of research and what they learned by showing their webs or other artifacts they created during their research. These informal presentations do not require significant preparation by students. Other times, research is shared through *formal presentations* to classmates, other classrooms, and/or parents. These presentations might include a published fiction or nonfiction book or piece of writing, mime, plays, choral readings, murals, songs, operas, masks, displays, oral presentations, paintings, sculpture, dramatizations, original musical compositions, diagrams, graphs, or charts.

In planning a formal presentation, students first consider their audience and make a list of what they think is most important to communicate about their inquiry to that audience. They then brainstorm a list of possible types

171

of presentations and focus on those that will best communicate their ideas. This process avoids the problem of students using a certain type of presentation, such as a skit, that may be popular in a classroom at a particular time but that may not be a good medium for communicating what they have learned through their inquiries. *Authors circles* (Short and Harste, with Burke 1996) can be a good place for students to take their in-process pieces of writing, artwork, and drama to share with a small group. In this setting they can revise their presentation to enhance its effectiveness.

Through sharing and presenting, students celebrate their understandings and demonstrate for others new strategies and possible topics for further inquiry. Presentations also encourage students to reflect on their current inquiries and plan new ones.

Planning New Inquiries

As students engage in inquiry, they need opportunities to reflect on what they know (content), how they come to know (process), and why they inquire (purpose and goals). The sharing and presentations pro-

vide an important context for students to take a reflexive stance as inquirers on how they approach learning. They can go beyond the immediate experience to broader meanings for their life. Following the presentations, it is essential to engage students in *group meetings*, where the class talks about what was learned about the processes and tools of inquiry and which of these might be used in other contexts. They also talk about their new understandings and how those understandings relate to broader sociopolitical issues in the world at large as well as to their personal lives in their own communities. An important part of these class discussions is a return to the original class webs and lists of questions and issues so as to reconsider them in light of students' inquiries.

Reflection can also be encouraged through *free writes*, *learning logs*, *reflection journals*, and *inquiry portfolios*, where students go through their journals, webs, sketches, questions, and other artifacts and select the items they consider to be most significant from their inquiry. These items are put into their portfolio and used to write a reflection about their learning. Another possibility is for students to compile a *reflection portfolio* (Kauffman and Short 1993) on who they are as learners. This encourages students to move beyond just gathering written artifacts for their portfolio. They bring objects from both school and home experiences and create tags for their self-reflections by using large Post-it notes. Through these reflections, students are able to examine their purposes as inquirers and establish goals for where they want to go next.

Taking Thoughtful New Action

The inquiry cycle is a never-ending process: as one set of inquiries comes together through presentations and reflection, a sense of where to go next emerges. Students end a particular inquiry experience with new questions about the topic they have been pursuing. Sometimes these questions become the basis of the new class inquiry focus, but other times the class is ready to move to a new focus. Even if a new focus is chosen, individual children can continue with the previous focus during *reading and writing work time*, which is reserved for children to pursue topics and issues of personal interest to them. Sometimes, a particular class focus does not emerge because students have such a wide range of questions and issues. In this case the class might move into individual and small-group *expert projects* (Copeland 1994; Smith 1992) or *Explorers' Clubs* (Copenhaver 1992).

To facilitate the decision of where to go next, the class returns to the *broad concept web* and adds new understandings or creates a new broad concept web to hang on the wall next to the older web. After adding their new understandings, students discuss where they might go next and again list possible topics, issues, and questions. Sometimes they return to the *exploration centers* on the broad concept to facilitate this process of curriculum negotiation.

While inquiries end with new understandings and questions, they should also lead students to take new actions in their lives. For example, if students engage in a study of human rights, this study should not lead just to presentations about human rights but to a discussion about the kinds of action students can take in their own lives and communities. These *action projects* might take the form of a class project, individual actions over a period of time, or changes in perspective. Action projects provide a point of connection so that students' school knowledge becomes part of the action knowledge that they use for living (Barnes 1976).

Conclusion

While the inquiry projects that students explore and present are exciting, it is important to remember that curriculum as inquiry starts with personal and social knowing (Short and Harste, with Burke 1996). This means that teachers begin the curriculum by listening, not by teaching. It also means that other learners play a key role and that a conducive environment for inquiry is a collaborative one.

Our focus as teachers is no longer on determining the information we need to teach but on offering students alternative perspectives on particular issues through sign systems, knowledge systems, and conversations. Instead of trying to teach students everything we think they need to know about a topic, we try to create environments that offer multiple perspectives and time to "wander and wonder" their way into inquiry. We are concerned with developing physical and social structures that encourage talk and interaction among students so they are encouraged to think collaboratively and critically with others in new ways.

We also believe that it is important to experience inquiry ourselves as teachers. Through our work as a group of teacher researchers, we have experienced firsthand what it feels like to wander and wonder and eventually find questions that we care about and can systematically investigate individually and collectively. Because we have had this experience ourselves, we better understand students' needs and experiences with inquiry.

Curriculum as inquiry is not simply an alternative to thematic units but a philosophy that permeates the entire school day (Harste 1992). Taking an inquiry perspective changed how we view the entire classroom learning environment as well as such specific issues as discipline, classroom organization, and approaches to reading and writing. Inquiry is not something we schedule into a certain time of the day; it is a belief system that underlies our thinking about the classroom and our lives as professionals. By using the inquiry cycle as our curricular framework, we have begun to put these beliefs about inquiry into action in our classrooms.

9 Time Marches On and So Do We: Continuing Our Research and Learning as Teachers

ONE OF THE key insights we gained from our research was an understanding of ourselves as learners. It is because we are learners that we continue to find teaching exciting and challenging. We learn, not because something is wrong with our classrooms or because we have a "deficit" as teachers, but because learning is synonymous with teaching. We agree with Carolyn Burke that a teacher is a "professional learner." There are always new questions and understandings for us to pursue about learning, teaching, and curriculum so that we can create even more powerful learning environments with our students.

Jerry Harste contends that it is through conversation that we outgrow our current selves. Our experiences have allowed us to see the generativeness of learning within communities of other educators and with our students. Throughout the "Discovery year" we continuously shared our learning process and questions with our students. We did not want research to be "done to" them, so we shared what we were doing and asked for their help in reflecting on their experiences. When an engagement seemed unproductive, we asked students to help us understand what was happening. The students knew that we met and talked with each other and came to expect that after our meetings we would come back to the classroom with new ideas, understandings, and questions to discuss with them. They were co-researchers as well as observers of our research process. We lived openly as learners in our classrooms.

In the previous chapters, we shared and reflected on our experiences as we explored inquiry and the broad concept of Discovery across our classroom contexts. These experiences marked a major turning point for all of us as we struggled to think in new ways about inquiry and curriculum. Since that year, we have continued meeting, talking, and working in our own classrooms in order to push our thinking theoretically and practically.

In this chapter, we reflect on some of our current thinking and classroom experiences and the questions we are continuing to explore. One of the factors that has influenced our thinking is that many of us have moved into multi-age and multi-year contexts. When we first began working together, most of us were teaching in traditional one-year grade level settings. Four years later, we have all moved to either a multi-age context, where children of two to three age levels share the same classroom over time, or a multi-year setting, where the entire classroom of students moves with the same teacher to the next grade.

Jean was already involved with, and enthusiastic about, multi-age settings through her experiences teaching six- to nine-year-olds in a primary multi-age classroom. More recently, she has been on leave from the school district for two years as a full-time graduate student. During that time she taught an undergraduate course for a year and the following year supervised some of the same students as student teachers to create a multi-year teaching context. Kathy continues to teach graduate courses at the university and has tried to schedule courses so that her students can move from one course to another connected course for the following semester in order to continue their inquiries.

Margaret has moved gradually from teaching first grade into a multi-age classroom for six- to eight-year-olds. Initially she continued teaching first grade, but teamed with the second-grade teacher so that half of her previous first graders came back as second graders in the mornings to create inquiry groups with half of her current first graders. She was impressed with the ways in which the second graders provided suggestions about the curriculum, planned strategies to support their learning, and made improvements in the daily routines. When she shared her enthusiasm and ideas with other teachers, the first- and second-grade teachers met and decided to reorganize into multi-age classrooms. This response to Margaret's sharing of new directions in her teaching made her aware of the importance of creating a community of learners for both students and teachers.

Both Gloria and Julie have taught in multi-year settings. Julie continued teaching kindergarten for several years but then had the opportunity to keep her students for a second year by following them into first grade. Gloria's fifth-grade students had been with her as fourth graders in a multi-year experience during the Discovery year. Since that time, she has taught a multi-age primary class and is now teaching an intermediate multi-age class that contains some of her primary students.

Kathleen took a one-year leave to be a full-time doctoral student at the university and then returned to teaching fourth grade in a new school. While she would have preferred to follow her entire class into fifth grade, she was assigned to an intermediate multi-age class, for the following year, so half of her students were able to continue with her in a new class setting.

Within each of these contexts, we have continued to think about classroom structures and strategies to help us deal with issues we feel are significant or problematic. These issues include listening to students' interests and questions, negotiating the curriculum focus with students, and integrating the use of a wide range of knowledge systems and sign systems into children's ongoing inquiry explorations. Although we feel that we have gained new understandings about these issues, we have lingering questions that we continue to examine as learners in our classrooms and in conversations with others. We know that our work with each other, other educators, and our students will continue to influence our thinking and learning as teachers.

Moving to Multi-Age and Multi-Year Classroom Settings

We see our shift to multi-age and multi-year settings not just as an organizational change but as a natural outgrowth of our interest in inquiry-based classrooms. We believe that these contexts encourage students to pursue their inquiries over longer periods of time within supportive communities (Chase and Doan 1994; Kasten and Clarke 1993).

One of the most obvious benefits of the multi-age and multi-year settings has been the carryover of relationships and knowledge of classroom routines. We found that establishing a sense of community at the beginning of the year or of a new course was a much smoother process because students already felt connected to each other and to us as teachers. Because of this comfort level, both we and our students were willing to take more risks in our own learning and in the curriculum we were creating together. Students were able to work more productively with each other and time was not lost learning new routines. On the first day of school, students came in, found their spaces, and sat down, ready to begin working and thinking with each other. Very little time was needed to discuss rules and routines because students knew what to expect. Not only do students more quickly form a community in multi-age and multi-year settings; they also bring experiences and understandings about the processes and strategies involved in taking an inquiry perspective on learning.

We realized that we had never appreciated as adults the trauma that some children feel about the constant change of teachers and classmates. Kathleen found the end of the year in fourth grade to be a particularly difficult experience when students learned who would remain in her classroom for the following year. One student shouted for joy after receiving his placement to remain in the class, while another broke into tears as he read his new placement in another class.

Multi-age settings allow students to continue their inquiries on particular issues during the following year. Toward the end of the Discovery year, Jean's students began to explore environmental issues. At the beginning of

Figure 9.1
*Reflection on Multi-age Classrooms
(Shelly, Age 7)*

179

the following year, it quickly became obvious that these issues were still of concern to them. They understood that negotiation was possible because of their previous experiences with Jean, and they immediately took a strong role in negotiating the curriculum.

Because students know they will continue in the same classroom setting, they can have a voice in planning for the following year and serve as experts in quickly orienting new students into the routines and expectations of the classroom. Margaret took advantage of this opportunity and at the end of the year discussed possible initiating events for the following school year with her students. Through these discussions, the class decided to continue the broad concept focus for a second year. They brainstormed initiating engagements that connected the broad focus and inquiry, suggested new room arrangements, and planned centers to welcome the new students the following year. This way, both Margaret and her students knew what to expect when the school year started. On registration day, returning students came in an hour before the new students and discussed their roles as mentors for the new students. As new students arrived, they were taken on a tour of the classroom, which gave all of the students a chance to get acquainted. Parents were invited to have lunch in the classroom and so were welcomed into the class community. Margaret noticed that the new students were comfortable the first few weeks of school because they had been introduced to the routines and had a returning student as a mentor. Returning students were proud of their role as mentors and worked to live up to the new students' expectations.

Kathleen's returning students explained the use of the classroom library, the location of writing tools, the assignment of jobs for the week, and other beginning-of-the-year routines that in previous years had been teacher directed. Returning students were quick to take responsibility when they noticed problems, such as books out of order in the library. They raised these issues in class meetings to help the new students understand the importance of the organization of the classroom.

We found that we benefited as teachers in a multi-age or multi-year setting because we already knew a great deal about our students both academically and personally. Julie noticed that she did not have to spend as much time on initial evaluations but could move immediately into the curriculum.

Gloria found that the more she understood her students and they understood the class procedures and expectations, the more she and her students could think together about curriculum that truly fit their needs. The curriculum became more powerful because meaningful connections were made with current experiences as well as with previous years.

Jean and Kathy believe that these same issues affect university courses, where students typically spend only one semester with a particular course and professor. They try to work with students over a more extended period of time. Jean found she was more effective as a student teacher supervisor with those students who had been in her undergraduate classes the previous year. Her understandings of their educational beliefs and their understandings of her beliefs facilitated their relationship, enhanced Jean's ability to support and push their thinking, and removed some of the anxiety that accompanies student teaching.

Kathy found the same advantages of a multi-year or semester format for graduate classes when she carefully scheduled her courses so that teachers could decide to move from one class to the next. The ability to sustain relationships and issues provided an effective and productive context for learning. While there were, of course, new class members, the continuing students quickly established a supportive learning community. Class members also moved more quickly into in-depth explorations of literacy and learning issues and often continued their projects from previous courses at a deeper level. Occasionally, voluntary "reunions" were scheduled. After a summer course on inquiry, for example, teachers from the course met on a Saturday morning in November and again in March to talk with each other about what was happening in their classrooms and to brainstorm ways to handle problems they were encountering.

Kathy has also explored a multi-age context at the university by scheduling a children's literature course so that one-third of the students are undergraduates and the rest of the class are master's and doctoral students. Because the course is a survey of children's literature and not a curriculum class, the range in background experiences is a positive factor. All class members respond as readers to each other in literature circles and dialogue journals. The undergraduate students bring an enthusiasm and fresh perspective to the course that graduate students find invigorating. The graduate students are able to connect the books to their own teaching experiences in ways that the undergraduate students find helpful. Both groups gain an appreciation of each other as people and as readers.

The depth of inquiries and the development of critical perspectives are major advantages of multi-age and multi-year settings. Instead of starting over and remaining at a broad overview level, students can build on relationships, previous content, and their learning strategies to examine more deeply issues about the world and their lives. We believe that one reason our group has been such a productive place for us to think is that we have been meeting for four years. We have developed a shared history and trusting relationships that we can use to critically address issues.

Listening to Our Students

While all of us were careful kidwatchers (Y. Goodman 1978) in our classrooms when we began working together, we found that finding better ways to listen to children was essential to creating curriculum with them (Pradl 1996). We needed to both listen to children as part of the regular ongoing activities of the classroom and create contexts that were specifically designed for us to listen to students. Our focus was not on teaching new ideas, but on setting up experiences so we could carefully observe and listen to children's understandings and questions. Because we spent so much time revisiting our classrooms by listening to tapes of children's discussions, we came to realize that their connections and questions were often much deeper than what we had initially thought as we sat in their groups. We knew we had to find more effective ways to really listen carefully to their ideas and issues.

Children continuously ask questions and wonder about their world as they engage in informal interactions and conversations. However, when we later ask them to list their questions, they often look at us blankly as if to say, "What's a question?" One explanation for this response may be that they are not aware that they are always asking questions. During initiating engagements at the beginning of the year, Margaret talked to students about what she heard them say to help them become more aware of their questions. She found that as she and her students gained experience listening, they were able to dig below the surface to find the deeper questions they were wondering about. Her students were gradually able to distinguish between factual questions they could easily answer in a reference source and questions that have more depth and could lead to an individual or small-group inquiry. This process has been gradual. Margaret feels that as she becomes a better listener, she is able to define her role as a listener to students and can help them learn how to listen to others and to reflect on their own thinking.

Margaret noticed that it was easier for her to listen when she was not actively participating in students' discussions. For example, when students had literature discussions and she could concentrate on listening, she was able to hear questions that were hidden or embedded in the dialogue. Often children asked a question and then continued with another idea without a pause, so she needed to listen carefully in order to hear those questions and be able to bring them up later for consideration. Another way we pull back from the frantic nature of classroom life and listen to students is to read students' written journals, stories, free writes, reflections, and self-evaluations. We also tape significant class or small-group discussions and listen to them later, often on the drive to or from school. As mentioned in Chapter 8, we also use large-class inquiry charts, learning logs, and slips of paper to encourage the continuous recording of student questions throughout their explorations.

As students wander and wonder, it is especially important for us to carefully watch and listen as students explore. We take field notes as children are engaged in exploration centers and note where they are spending their time, what seems to be of most interest to them, and what kinds of conversations are occurring.

Although we listen carefully to students, we do not assume that we have really "heard" them and that our hypotheses about what they are saying match their thinking. We often talk to students about what we think we hear them say and ask whether or not these issues are ones they are thinking about and, if so, whether those issues are important to them and worth pursuing further. As we walk around and observe students working individually or in small groups, we not only note our observations but we often ask students, "What are you doing?" or "What are you thinking in your mind?" These questions come out of our genuine interest in their thinking. Not surprisingly, what seems obvious to us is often *not* what students perceive is occurring. Another effective strategy is to gather for a class meeting after work time and ask students to share what they were doing and thinking. As they share, we listen and take notes about their explanations of what they were doing and the processes they were using to learn.

The interview that we developed and used in the fall and spring of the Discovery year was initially introduced as a research tool for us to examine students' understandings about history and perspective. However, we quickly realized that it played a very important function in allowing us to step back and listen carefully to students' understandings before continuing with an inquiry focus. The small-group experiences and discussions that were part of the interview process provided Julie with a different way to learn about her students' understandings and experiences. She found that none of her students had heard of Christopher Columbus and that their concepts of time order and events in history were limited. She used their responses to make decisions about curriculum. She wanted to expand on their knowledge of history, and the interviews gave her an idea of where to start. She continues to adapt this interview to explore her students' understandings of class studies. For example, as part of a study of friendship, her students became interested in exploring the issue of self-control. They met in small groups with Julie to web "What is self-control?" and then talked as a class about the ways in which their small-group webs were alike and different in their conceptions of self-control. This brainstorming and discussion gave Julie a much better sense of students' conceptions and encouraged students to begin their inquiry by connecting to what they already knew.

Gloria also continues to use the engagements that were part of our interview as a tool for listening to, observing, and understanding her students as learners. These engagements are much more than just asking children to web what they know. While she wants to gain an understanding of their knowledge base, she also wants to observe the strategies that they are already using as learners. The interview is not a set of isolated activities, but engagements that help children explore the broad concept, build strategies for inquiry, and begin to consider the content they want to study later in greater depth. She also makes sure that she does not just listen to what the children are saying, but asks herself why they might be engaging in particular behaviors or thinking. She can then pull back and reflect with the class and with individuals on what they were thinking about during the engagement, as well as their process for planning their work.

One engagement that Gloria added to the interview is to move from webbing, reflecting, and exploring the broad concept into mini-inquiries at the beginning of the year. These mini-inquiries last for only one week, but they introduce the inquiry cycle to students and they allow Gloria to observe students' inquiry strategies. For example, as students explored the broad concept of Storying About Our World and Lives, they kept a list of connections and issues that interested them. From this list, five groups were formed: color; toads; Anne Frank; teenagers and drugs; and Mexican culture. Students used interviews, artifacts, literature, observation, and experimentation to quickly explore their questions within these topics. Through her observations, Gloria noted that students had effective strategies for exploring a topic, finding diverse connections, and asking individual questions, but had difficulty developing and researching a shared question as a group. The class used their mini-inquiries to talk about the inquiry cycle, to continue their discussions about the broad concept, and to negotiate their first class focus.

Kathy uses many of these same small-group processes at the beginning of her courses or in workshops with teachers. She asks teachers to web or graffiti their understandings of a broad concept, such as Story or Literacy or Sense of Place, that relates to the focus of the course or workshop. As part of these explorations she often asks them to read a short story as partners using Say Something (Short and Harste, with Burke 1996), construct and share time lines of significant life events related to the concept, bring artifacts about their sense of place or an important story in their lives, and orally share stories about their own lives that relate to the course focus. Through the sharing and webs, she gains a sense of her students' personal and professional experiences and what is significant to them.

Kathleen uses the interview process at the beginning of every year to set up experiences so she can listen to students' understandings about the broad concept. She has added frequent free writes on students' thoughts and connections to the interview. One year the class's broad concept was Harmony. She asked students where they saw harmony in particular read-alouds or where they saw harmony in the school cafeteria or playground games. She planned engagements so that students could explore and think about how they understood harmony.

Throughout these engagements, Kathleen keeps field notes and student artifacts, such as webs, lists, and reflections, so she can examine what students believe about the broad concept. The questions students ask about the broad concept reflect their understandings. This process allows students to determine their own meanings for the broad concept, just as students did in each of our classrooms for Discovery. Sometimes through this process, it becomes apparent that the broad concept is not significant to the students and that another theme is running through their comments and needs to become the broad concept.

Negotiating Curriculum with Students

One of our central concerns about inquiry has been how to really negotiate curriculum *with* our students and not just build curriculum *from* our students. While we have become better kidwatchers who listen to, and build from, children's needs and interests, we want more. We want to really think through these curricular decisions with children in ways that are meaningful and productive for them. We want our classrooms to be based in democracy and in children's having a voice in the "behind the scenes" decisions and listing of choices (Edelsky 1994; Shannon 1993). We believe that in order for this negotiation to be productive, students need a supportive context so they can connect to, and go beyond, their previous experiences. We have searched for engagements and structures that will support children in this kind of curricular decision-making.

Julie has gradually found ways to give young children more freedom to choose their own activities and make decisions. She believes that these changes have come from learning to listen more carefully to her students and from giving them the time they need to explore, connect, and wonder. In the past, she asked her students on the first day of school, "What do you want to learn?" Their answers were never what she hoped would emerge but ranged from the generic "learn to read" and "learn to do math" to "I want to make things." Generally, once one student talked about learning to make something (for example, an airplane), she would be inundated with responses of what other students wanted to learn to make. While students did share their ideas, she didn't feel that the web of their responses was helpful in defining the curriculum. The list consisted of isolated topics or activities because the students lacked a context for the brainstorming.

Julie no longer asks students what they want to learn on the first day of school. She also doesn't begin a particular unit of study by asking, "What do you know?" and "What do you want to know?" Instead she provides more time for wandering and wondering. During this time, she closely observes students and listens to their responses. Her students explore through listening to read-aloud books, participating in exploration centers, and engaging in field study and imaginative play. The class does make a web of what students want to learn about a topic, but not until they have had time to explore and share.

Since Margaret has become more aware of the importance of students' own questions, she constantly looks for structures and situations that will encourage them to voice those questions. She sees their questions as essential for developing the curriculum but initially was not sure how to center the curriculum around their questions. The year after the Discovery focus, she started with a predetermined curriculum for the first half of the year but kept track of students' questions as they came up. During the second semester, the students' own questions were used to form eight inquiry groups that lasted the entire semester. One of her realizations from this experience was the importance of pushing students to move from factual questions to more in-depth conceptual questions. The groups who stayed with easily answered questions pursued activities that were concrete and product oriented and ended up only with a collection of facts. This experience provided the transition she needed in order to focus the entire curriculum around students' own questions the following year.

Our experiences with Discovery convinced us that broad concepts could provide a supportive context for negotiating curriculum with students. We began working with Discovery because it was a way to connect our classrooms and allow us to plan and think together even though we taught in different schools with students of different ages. Through our conversations and experiences, we found that the broad concept played an increasingly important role in providing a supportive context within which we could think and negotiate with our students. We have each continued to work with the broad concept and with thinking through structures that will facilitate the negotiation of curriculum with our students.

Margaret starts the school year by having students explore the broad concept and create lists of possible questions at the same time they are becoming acquainted and forming a community. By the middle of the first quarter, the class is working together to choose a more specific focus for a class study related to the broad concept. Because of her multi-age context, she is able to meet with her students to discuss the broad concept for the following year so that students have a voice in this decision.

One year her students decided to continue with the broad concept of Bridges the following year but with a particular focus on friendship issues. As they explored friendship broadly at the beginning of the year, she wrote down their questions on a large chart. The class then used the chart in a whole-group meeting to create categories based on which questions seemed to go together. Throughout this process of asking questions, categorizing, and negotiating with young children, Margaret finds she needs to listen and reflect back to them what she thinks they might be saying. When discussing friendship, questions about cooperating with others in creating a garden in the school courtyard came up frequently. Margaret pointed out this recurring theme to her students and asked whether this issue was one they wanted to explore through further inquiry. Because of their prior experiences with her, students knew that her question was a genuine one and that they could offer alternative suggestions. In this case, they decided that these issues were the most significant to them at that point and moved into a combined focus on gardening and cooperation.

Julie found that negotiating the curriculum the second year with the same students was a much easier process. They started where they had left off the previous year. In kindergarten, they had focused on Change in themselves and their families. They began first grade by returning to their web on the broad concept of Change and decided on a focus on friends. After each class study, Julie and her students came back to their large web on Change to see what they wanted to add. They talked about the other areas on the web and revisited some of their exploration centers on Change while Julie observed carefully to see what they might be interested in exploring. While older students are often able to state and negotiate their issues and topics directly, Julie finds that with young children she usually needs to observe and listen and then introduce an option and see how students respond to her suggestions.

Gloria uses a broad concept to focus her thinking about the curriculum and to identify possible connections that might run across the day and year before school begins. She then sets up engagements so that children can explore and develop their understandings of the concept. Through those experiences, she listens to the connections children are sharing. She often uses literature to encourage children to make their own connections and to build from these connections as a source of information and stories as they move into more focused inquiry. She gathers information on the children's connections through observing them and asking them to reflect on their learning processes. These observations and reflections become the basis for negotiating the next focus of the curriculum.

To include more of the children's voices directly in this process of negotiation, Gloria asks children to record their topics, issues, and questions about a particular concept, book, or theme. For example, when children explored the broad concept of Connections, they browsed through exploration centers that contained books and artifacts on themes such as culture, time and history, war and peace, inventions, bones, memories, musical stories, patterns, money, homes, the homeless, and environments over time. Gloria also engaged the children in several whole-class experiences around the broad concept. She took field notes and reflected with the class on their explorations to give her insights into their current strategies as learners.

After spending a week browsing and sharing from these centers, students took several days to again visit the centers, but this time they recorded their topics, issues, and questions on small slips of paper. They then sat in small groups and sorted these slips of paper into different piles to create categories of related ideas and topics, such as invasion, racism, movement, health, rebuilding, memories, patterns, start to finish, and struggles. These categories were combined to create a class web on connections. Students used this web to further negotiate which of these categories they wanted to choose for their class focus by talking about which categories interested them and why. By carefully listening and talking with each other, they were able to decide on their first class focus.

During the year when her class is ready to move into a new class focus, Kathleen asks her students to reflect on their new understandings of the broad concept based on the study they have just finished. They first return to their web on the broad concept to see what they want to add and if they need to reorganize the web in any way. They then create free writes on what the broad concept means to them personally and the questions and issues that they find interesting or significant. They use these free writes to pull out topics, issues, and questions that might become part of the next class study by sharing in small groups with other class members. As categories of the topics, issues, and questions are formed in their small groups, students learn how to negotiate with each other by making decisions and coming to agreement on their newly formed categories.

In reflecting on this process of negotiating in Kathleen's classroom, Lacy wrote that it involves "combining things together" to come to agreement. Josh stated, "We decide how they all go together and if they all go together we have one group, and if they don't then maybe we have more then one group." The categories formed in the small groups are shared with the class so each person's perspectives and understandings are heard by all class members. Kathleen makes sure that all students have time to share their ideas before beginning to negotiate the new focus. She wants to avoid situations in which the loudest or first voice determines what will happen next.

Kathleen and Gloria believe that this process gives children a stronger voice in decisions about the class focus because they have a tool for sorting, grouping, and categorizing their thoughts. The topics, issues, and questions help the class negotiate a common agreement instead of voting on a topic. Voting seems to lead to winners and losers, and some children feel angry about the class choice. The process of creating categories and sharing *why* they think a particular category would be a good focus of study encourages children to think more deeply about their choice. Often their choice is not any of the original categories, but a new category that is created through their discussions with each other.

When Gloria and her students discussed a class focus based on Connections, they used the web of their categories to talk in small groups about what they wanted to study as a class. Initially when the small groups came to the class meeting, each group had chosen a different category for what they wanted to study next. However, because they shared both their choice and the reason behind their choice, the class was able to focus on the reasons why groups wanted to study a particular topic, and those discussions led to a new broad concept and a class focus that was not on the original web of categories. They decided that the broad concept of Connections was not powerful for them and changed the concept to Living a Better Life. This decision then led them into a specific class study on immigration.

All of us have found that sometimes the new class focus does not require such an involved process of negotiation because that focus becomes evident as students give presentations and pull together the previous focus. Even in this case, we still take time to return to the web of the broad concept. Some of us create a new web on the concept each time because we've found that the categories and topics change so much. Each web is hung on the wall next to the previous one. Others have students add to the existing web each time. Even though the class may already have decided on the next focus, we want to encourage them to view their focus within a broader context.

Kathleen did not want to choose the broad concept for the new school year without inviting her returning students to be part of the process. At the end of the year, students again wrote free writes on the class broad concept of Harmony and the issues that were still significant to them. They also pulled together portfolios of themselves as learners and used these to write self-evaluations about their learning. For example, ten-year-old Thea wrote the following reflection:

> I know that harmony sometimes means stopping bad things like abuse and other bad things like that. I know that harmony means helping stop bad things and not just letting everybody else do the hard work. You have got to help our world have lots more harmony or we would be better off living with the devil. I think harmony is also making friends and even the people you don't like, you should try to get along with them. I also think that harmony means making our world a better place to live around. I also know that harmony means to be nice to one another. It means not littering and helping

other people like cross streets and helping other people do things you know they need help with. I think harmony is PEACE!!!!!!!!!!

I will try to pick up litter on the ground and also try to recycle, feed the birds, and keep other people's spirits up by keeping everybody joyful at the right times and in the right places. I will also try to end war and violence and things that should not belong in our world. I will write letters to TV programs so that they can learn that people are dying and fighting because of the violent shows. I can also help by telling doctors that people really need help and you should take lots more people in than one person at a time in three hours.

As Kathleen read through their free writes and self-evaluations, student comments about making a difference in the world appeared over and over, so she proposed this as the broad concept for the following year.

Kathleen, Jean, and Kathy have all used the broad concept in university classes to support some negotiation of the curriculum. For example, in a course on children's literature, Kathleen had preservice teachers read a shared book, *Bridge to Terabithia* (Paterson 1977), and web their understandings of Change. These webs were used to create categories of themes and issues related to Change, and students joined inquiry groups to develop text sets around their different issues about Change.

One of the frustrations in a university context are the time limitations of meeting once or twice a week for one semester and the difficulty of finding the time to really negotiate curriculum with students. Kathy sets up the first half of the semester so that teachers in her graduate courses can explore the course focus broadly from many perspectives. At midterm she asks class members to develop a focus for their course projects and negotiate the issues they want to explore in greater depth during the remainder of the semester. Often projects are still in process at the end of the semester, so she has developed alternative ways for class members to pull their work together. For example, class members often turn in a project notebook, which includes their field notes, classroom artifacts, related readings, an informal paper in which they write about what they did and learned, reflections on their learning, and plans for how they will continue their inquiries once the course ends. She also identifies courses the following semester that will allow them to continue their inquiries and encourages groups that have worked well together to continue to meet as a study group to support each other as teachers.

In negotiating curriculum with students, additional factors often need to be taken into account. The school district and state curricula have not been a major issue for us because we have found ways to integrate these areas into the broad concept and connect them to children's interests and concerns. A topic may be addressed in a slightly different way, such as Gloria's fifth graders' study of slavery instead of the standard unit on the Civil War, Margaret's and Julie's students' focus on changes in families instead of the usual first-grade unit on family, and Kathleen's fourth-grade study of Arizona from the perspective of culture. In examining the mandated curriculum, we found that many times the specific topics are not actually mandated but are just traditions at a particular grade level. For example, it may have become a tradition that third graders do a unit on Japan when the mandated curriculum simply calls for a focus on world cultures. The mandated curriculum often consists of general areas and concepts that we can integrate into various class foci. Also, not all children have to study each topic in depth and have the same experiences. Children can learn about some topics by listening to presentations from other groups.

Sometimes, however, we find that certain mandated topics are difficult to integrate into ongoing inquiry. Our focus on time and culture through Discovery meant that some of the mandated science topics were not relevant. As can be seen from the daily schedules at the conclusion of Chapters 3–7, many of us have a time period several times a week where these topics are addressed through short-term class studies.

Another factor that affects curriculum negotiation is student teachers. While student teachers add to the classroom learning environment in positive ways, they also can constrain the curriculum. Student teachers often have no background in inquiry through their methods courses and so are unsure of how to operate within our classrooms. The university requirement that student teachers develop and teach a thematic unit is a major obstacle to the children continuing their ongoing inquiry. The unit has to be turned into the university a month before it is actually taught; this is not possible in classrooms where teachers and students negotiate the topic of study. Another problem is that the unit requirements involve listing activities and objectives separately by subject areas. The result has been that student teachers often end up doing twice the amount of work because they develop the unit for the university but teach something different based on what is negotiated with children. Other times the class stops its inquiry and "takes a break" while the student teacher teaches the planned unit. While this approach is easier for the student teacher, it is confusing for the children and often means that the class has to start over by returning to the broad concept and brainstorming to redevelop the concept and where they might go next.

One year, Kathleen found that after the student teacher had taught her thematic unit on the environment, the students kept raising questions about the environment. They had negotiated another topic for a class focus, but when questions about the environment kept coming up in class discussions, Kathleen realized that the unit had given them information the student teacher thought was important about the environment. The structure of the thematic unit, however, had not allowed them to pursue their own questions, so they decided to drop the class focus that had been decided earlier and spend more time on their own questions on the environment.

Another factor that can influence negotiation is working with other teachers at the same grade level in a school. The kindergarten teachers at Julie's school have always had a collegial relationship and meet together to do most of their curriculum planning. Because Julie values her relationship with these teachers and their expertise in different areas, she has continued to plan with them. There are times, however, when the group plans do not match her students' interests and so, while she continues to meet and think with the group, she develops a different curricular plan in her classroom from the topics her colleagues are pursuing in their classrooms.

We need to remind ourselves that negotiation is a two-way street. Students must be willing to enter into thinking and planning with teachers. Sometimes new students have only experienced teacher-directed classrooms, and they have difficulty making choices and setting their own directions. "Just tell me what to do" is a familiar refrain. Just as teachers operate on a set of beliefs about learning and teaching, so do students, and an inquiry-based curriculum can be in direct opposition to their beliefs about schooling.

Sign Systems and Knowledge Systems

Our work with inquiry convinced us that we needed to understand more about ways to include the multiple perspectives of knowledge systems and the multiple ways to create and share meaning through sign systems. We wanted to get beyond just setting up centers or activities to highlight a particular knowledge or sign system. These perspectives and ways of meaning-making needed to become a natural part of classroom life and thinking. Our students constantly use reading and writing as they go about their inquiries, not through a special activity, but as part of their thinking and sharing with others. We wanted that same natural integration to cut across a wider range of knowledge and sign systems.

Jean found that her awareness of sign systems and knowledge systems greatly increased her recognition of the complexities of teaching. She became convinced that new understandings about children's questions are often readily available, but that teachers need ways to see and hear those new perspectives. During the Discovery focus, her class became fascinated with history. Their explorations helped Jean understand the potential of knowledge systems and a broad range of perspectives on any topic or issue. She now observes situations from alternate perspectives, and what she might previously have dismissed as irrelevant now catches her attention. No matter what the topic, she tries to use materials and resources that reflect multiple perspectives and searches out primary sources to support children's inquiries.

Recently Jean was an observer in a fifth-grade class during a math lesson where students were using base-ten sets. A block representing 1,000 units was introduced to a small group and they were asked how many units made up the block. The girl holding the large cube bonked it against her head, confirming for herself that the light weight of the object was indeed due to its being hollow. She then counted the number of sides, knowing that each side was 100 units, and concluded that the block consisted of 600 units. While the teacher explained that it was intended to represent 1,000 units, Jean found herself planning an investigation of production costs and retail sales, decision-making, representation, and symbolism. She asked herself curriculum planning questions such as who could we ask, how could we try this in class, could an expert come in and help, and what were the factors in deciding to manufacture the product in this way. The richness that exists within any learning context has become much more evident to all of us.

The different viewpoints on the Columbus event made Margaret more careful about including multiple perspectives on topics her students examine. She encourages them to discuss alternative meanings and use their different perspectives to understand each other and broaden their learning. She continues to read *Best Friends* (Kellogg 1986) at the start of each school year to promote discussion of different perspectives. After reading *Building a Bridge* (Begaye 1993) to her students, they talked about feeling "different" in a classroom. Children shared personal experiences and talked about issues of skin color. This experience promoted an in-depth exploration of differences in families and cultural experiences. Because of this experience, Margaret thinks very carefully about the books she reads aloud and the tools she introduces to promote discussion and the consideration of other perspectives.

Margaret's investigations of knowledge systems has focused on the use of primary sources as an important way of learning. She continues to invite many people into the classroom to share their experiences and expertise with the students. Her class goes on field studies to learn within environments other than the classroom. The students' interest in the rain forest and their trip to the botanical gardens led to a realization that while it may not always be possible to actually observe the real situation, students can still become involved in a simulation or share in another person's experiences.

In order to bring in such a wide range of perspectives, we find that we need the help of librarians, parents, and outside experts. Librarians can be a major support when children are involved in in-depth research and inquiry, especially when student topics are diverse and student groups need help to keep everyone working productively. Difficulties may arise, however, when librarians direct children into a research model based on finding basic facts to present instead of exploring to find ideas and information for their own inquiries.

All of us have worked at encouraging students to make and share meaning through a wider range of sign systems. Because of our own comfort levels, however, we each tend to encourage several systems at the expense of others (Eisner 1994). Still, we want students to see that they have choices in the ways they express themselves. In the past, meanings that children expressed through movement or art were considered significant only when a child didn't fit the "norm" and could not easily use reading and writing to learn. Now we consider the role of sign systems in learning and respect all children's efforts at making and expressing meaning.

When Margaret demonstrates a particular strategy involving a sign system to students, such as Sketch to Stretch (Short and Harste, with Burke 1996), she always discusses the reasons why that strategy might be useful. Once children are aware of the role that particular strategies or procedures can play in their thinking, they are able to make decisions about when to use these systems in their own presentations and learning.

Kathleen finds that many of her current questions involve trying to think through how to incorporate sign systems into the classroom. She wonders what a classroom looks like where sign systems are encouraged as part of the meaning-making in the curriculum and not simply another activity. She is concerned about where to find resource people (artists, musicians, etc.) to support the students' understandings. After reading *Carolina Shout!* (Schroeder 1995), a book about a little girl who hears music in all she does throughout the day, Adrian said to the class, "That's how I feel all the time too! I hear music all day long in all I do." Adrian's comment led Kathleen to wonder how she could get the resources to support Adrian's understanding of meaning through music and where thirty students could find the space to work within their own particular sign system without distracting others.

Gloria includes many perspectives on the broad concept through the materials and artifacts included in exploration centers so children are introduced to multiple ways of thinking. Children are encouraged to think like scientists or architects in order to acquire a new view of a topic or issue. As children create and share their understandings, Gloria makes many tools available for them to express those understandings. Children are able to use art, music, movement, drama, and mathematics to express their ideas. Recently she realized that in order to express themselves through multiple sign systems, children must come in contact with people that use those sign systems to make sense of their world. She has invited artists and other professionals to come to the classroom and engage in their process of thinking with children.

Multiple sign systems should be available at all times for students to think through ideas and not just to present their work at the end of their research. Gloria used to ask students to write about their ideas and keep written notes as they explored and researched, but now she encourages them to use sketches as well as writing in their notes, brainstorming, and observations. They also continuously use webs, graffiti boards, diagrams, and flow charts as they observe and research.

Gloria has become convinced that children need to have sustained time working in a particular sign system in order to become comfortable and fluent in that system as well as to explore the potential of that system. Writing workshop and authoring cycle approaches provide time to explore writing as a sign system. For the last several years, Gloria has scheduled studio time every Friday morning. The studio lasts the entire morning, so children know they have a large chunk of time for exploring and creating. During studio, children can use any sign system—art, music, movement, drama, language, mathematics—to create meaning. Areas with tools for the different sign systems have been established—a keyboard with earphones, listening centers with music tapes, mathematical blocks and geoboards, books, writing papers and utensils, art materials and papers, and dress-up clothing and puppets. Her students create a plan on Thursday afternoons for how they will schedule their time the next day and list what they plan to do and why. (Figure 9.2 shows an example of one student's planning and reflection.) They begin Friday morning with a class meeting to talk about their goals for studio and then move to the different areas of the classroom. At various points throughout the morning, children share what they are working on with each other in small groups, and the morning ends with a whole-group sharing. Some children have established long-term projects in a particular sign system that they work on every Friday morning; others move across many sign systems, exploring different possibilities.

The sign system that we and other educators have most struggled with integrating into ongoing inquiry is mathematics. We are convinced that mathematics is a part of how we think about the world and occurs all the

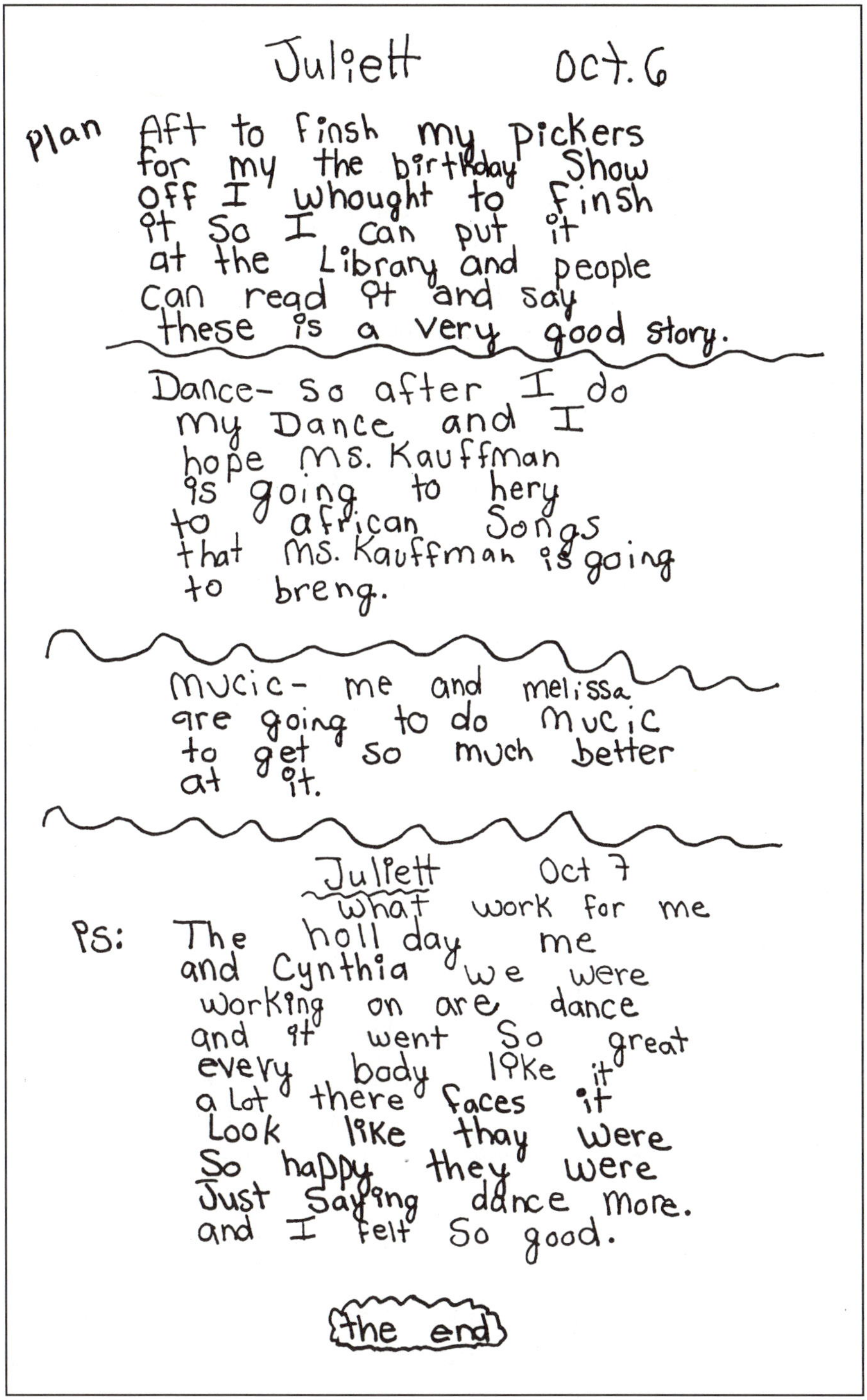

Juliett   Oct. 6

Plan Aft to finsh my pickers
      for my the birthday Show
      off I whought to finsh
      it So I can put it
      at the Library and people
      can read it and say
      these is a very good story.

      Dance- so after I do
      my Dance and I
      hope Ms. Kauffman
      is going to hery
      to african Songs
      that Ms. Kauffman is going
      to breng.

      Mucic- me and melissa
      are going to do mucic
      to get So much better
      at it.

            Juliett   Oct 7
            what work for me
PS: The holl day me
     and Cynthia we were
     working on are dance
     and it went So great
     every body like it
     a lot there faces it
     Look like thay were
     So happy they were
     Just Saying dance more.
     and I felt So good.

            the end

Figure 9.2
*Studio Planning and
Reflection (Juliett,
Age 11)*

time, but that most of us fail to identify that thinking as mathematics because we associate math with computations and word problems (Hornstein 1994; Whitin, Mills, and O'Keefe 1990). We have worked at mathematics as a sign system in a number of ways. One is to emphasize contextual math, where children use mathematics as part of the daily jobs of the classroom, such as taking attendance and lunch count, filling out book orders, and noting the date and the temperature. We constantly watch for opportunities to highlight mathematical thinking in children's inquiries through whole-class engagements, small-group activities, experience centers, and resource speakers. Since students often do not consider this thinking as math, we frequently point out instances of mathematical thinking in children's discussions and engagements throughout the day.

Most of us also have a time period that focuses on mathematics several times a week, just as we also have writing work times to highlight writing processes. During these math work times, children engage in mathematical explorations using manipulatives, and we teach mathematical strategy lessons (Hornstein 1994). We also engage students in test-taking skills of mathematical facts that they need to know for standardized tests. In addition, we continue to read and talk with others to increase our own understanding of mathematics as a sign system because we believe there are many more opportunities where we could integrate mathematics that we now miss and will be able to see once we understand more about this sign system.

Thinking and Learning with Other Educators

Thinking, planning, and reflecting on curriculum as a group of educators was a new experience for many of us. While we had all worked with other educators in many different projects, planning and reflecting on curriculum had remained essentially an individual process. All of us were innovative and effective teachers working and planning by ourselves, but by thinking with each other we were able to push ourselves to new understandings and possibilities that went far beyond what we could each do alone. We spent a year planning and reflecting on what was happening in our classrooms and then spent three years trying to make sense of those experiences. The luxury of having this time with each other is something we all value highly.

While the group initially was an important place for planning to plan as a teacher, it has become less so as students have become a stronger part of the curriculum negotiation process in our classrooms. We do continue to talk with each other individually and to talk about broad concepts and ideas as a group. We share and celebrate the changes and the new ideas each of us is exploring. As we talk to colleagues at other schools who are committed to inquiry and who are struggling without the support of a group, we realize how important the group has been for our growth as teachers. Being part of a group gave us support and encouragement as inquirers and learners, and we continue to share ideas, results, and new directions. As we continue thinking together, we have maintained the same commitment to inquiry that we ask of our students.

Engaging in a teacher research project takes a great deal of personal discipline because of the time needed to reflect and to continue gathering and analyzing data. The group helped us maintain this discipline. Because we meet at least once a month and establish goals for what we will do before the next meeting, these deadlines keep us focused on the project. We may not meet every deadline, but at least we keep working toward our goals.

We didn't fully realize the importance of the group in our thinking and planning as teachers until the following year, when our meetings focused on the previous research year. Jean found that the next school year seemed incredibly lonely. For over a year, the "Columbus group" (as we called ourselves) had met and collaborated. While we created different curricula in our own classrooms during that year, we were strongly connected by our efforts to understand and implement inquiry and our common broad concept. The support the group provided was a new experience for Jean, and she didn't realize its power until later. When our talk moved to analyzing data from the previous year, Jean missed the support for what was currently happening in her classroom. She found webbing possibilities, brainstorming titles, and reflecting hollow experiences when her voice was the only one.

During that year, Jean wanted to see if she could apply what she had learned about inquiry on her own. Now she realizes that she was still acting on the belief that a teacher must be able to implement an approach alone in order to be judged effective. Instead of building new understandings, she found herself trying to replicate the curriculum of the preceeding year, just by herself this time. Her theoretical understandings about inquiry had grown, but she was asking an outdated question about practice. Now she believes that having the support of others is not a weakness but a strength. She had spent the previous year talking about her classroom in new ways with us, and we were willing to hear the gory details of everyday life. She found that by trying to replicate the previous year, she remained too safe in her practice, instead of pushing herself as she had before. She also realized the importance of choosing a substantive question to ask as a teacher researcher each year.

As we continue to reflect on inquiry and our classrooms, understandings that we had not previously been able to express in words have taken shape and meaning. We are still creating new understandings about what happened during the research year. As mentioned earlier, we had initially intended the fall and spring interviews to be simply a way to measure growth in the children's understanding. Through our reflections, we realized that these interviews were a powerful tool for listening to children. Though we no longer share the specifics of what we are doing in our classrooms in our meetings, the overwhelming support of the group continues to enhance our understandings of inquiry. Because of our experiences in the group, reflection and listening are now essential to our everyday professional lives.

Being part of the support group gave Margaret confirmation of her changing role as a teacher. We created similar learning environments, explored the potential of talk within our classrooms, and spent many hours discussing our roles and the roles of the students. Through this talk, Margaret feels that she is better able to analyze the process of learning and teaching and is aware of students' questions as they develop. She values the sharing of strategies for inquiry and feels that the responses of group members to her ideas encourage her to keep growing and learning.

Julie feels that working with a support group was essential for her. She often felt frustrated and would have found it easy to say, "This doesn't work with kindergarten children," and abandon the project. Each meeting she brought up her frustrations and feelings of inadequacy when other group members talked about their students forming inquiry groups and working on personal inquiries. She needed the group to tell her that she was doing inquiry with her students. While kindergartners may not form groups and work individually or without adult support, they can still work within an inquiry curriculum. We offered suggestions and strategies she could try in her classroom, but more important, we provided positive support and confirmed that what she was doing was OK.

Kathy noticed a change in the thinking and contributions that she made to the group and how that influenced her work with teachers. Initially, the discussions focused around the experiences with children, which made her think through how she might use these ideas as part of her university teaching or in workshops with teachers. The work in elementary classrooms informed her teaching with adults. Over time, however, as she found ways to work with broad concepts and negotiate curriculum with adults, she shared her ideas. Her work with adults then informed the other group members' work in elementary classrooms. For example, Kathy became concerned that by bringing books already organized into text sets, she was not giving participants enough voice in the "behind the scenes" decisions. Participants chose the text set they wanted to discuss, but she determined the sets. She began to bring in many different books that were related to the broad concept and to put these out, unorganized, as part of her students' exploration of the broad concept. Once the participants had created their own webs of the broad concept with categories of possible topics and issues, they used these ideas to sort the books into text sets. The sharing and adaptation of ideas became a two-way process, where the teachers of adults and the teachers of children informed each other in thought-provoking ways.

The group's discussions were important to Gloria because she constantly looks for opportunities to discuss what she is doing and thinking with others who share similar beliefs about learning. This sharing gives her time to reflect on her curriculum in order to improve her teaching. These discussions also help her determine possible future directions for her curriculum. For many years she has met with colleagues to discuss curriculum and classroom life. She has also had several experiences working closely with others on projects that relate directly to her classroom. These collaborative opportunities have pushed her to consider whether her teaching practices fit her theoretical beliefs about learning.

The Columbus group was a focused study group that was different from occasional sharing with others. As a study group we determined a common focus and planned experiences that were similar across our classrooms. The sharing was much more intense. We did not have to give background information on our classrooms, our beliefs, and our students to each other. We were not put in the position of being experts and presenting to each other. We reflected together and built on one another's ideas. These ideas were not just activities we had done in the past and were passing on to each other. We had to create new engagements to meet the needs of our students. Our group came to know one another's students as thinkers, so we could consider the voices of the children from our different contexts as we talked about curriculum. Planning together, gathering materials, and reflecting on a continual basis contributed to a powerful support system and to a deeper level of thinking and critiquing our beliefs and practices.

Part of the reason we came together so quickly as a group was that many of us had previously taken courses at the university and collaborated on different class projects. Working as a research group built on, and took us beyond, these initial relationships. Because Kathleen valued our discussions, she wanted the conversations about creating curriculum with her students to continue on a regular basis. When we began to meet less frequently to focus on data analysis, Kathleen knew that she wanted to continue meeting regularly with a group of teacher researchers. She joined a group of primary teachers who were just beginning to use broad concepts to generate inquiry with their students. This group of kindergarten and first-grade teachers formed after hearing our research group share our experiences in a university course. They met twice a month for a year to discuss their classrooms and how they saw the broad concept and inquiry in their primary classrooms. The group also presented at local conferences on inquiry in the primary grades. One of the first-grade teachers moved to fourth grade, and she and Kathleen continue to meet every two weeks to discuss their classrooms. Making time to collaborate with other teachers has become a necessity in Kathleen's teaching, so she can talk about what she sees as she and her students negotiate curriculum. The other teachers she talks with give her support and encouragement to continue on her journey of exploring curriculum and learning.

The significance of our group in encouraging and pushing us as learners and teachers has been evident when we talk with other teachers in university classes and at conferences. While teachers are interested in our experiences with inquiry and the kinds of engagements and structures we have used in our classrooms, they always express envy of our group and our relationships with each other. One of the most frequent responses has been the formation of their own small groups to meet and think together. Given the time pressures and frantic lifestyles of most teachers, we believe that their initiative in forming a groups to meet on a regular basis speaks clearly to the need we all share for learning within a supportive community.

Conclusion

In reflecting on our learning throughout this process of working and thinking, we see ourselves moving through an inquiry cycle as adult learners. We built on our previous work in our own classrooms, particularly our experiences with thematic units and our earlier conversations with each other. We began to explore history, time, culture, and perspective only to find that tensions arose as we tried to establish supportive learning environments for children to examine these concepts. These tensions led us to ask questions about how to establish a curriculum that supports inquiry. We talked, read, went to conferences, tried engagements in our classrooms, and talked some more. These broad explorations led each of us into different focused inquiries in our classroom settings as we tried to work out the concept of curriculum as inquiry for ourselves. Our individual inquiries, however, were always supported by our collaboration with each other, and we were constantly challenged to consider other perspectives by our conversations. We reflected on our experiences through teaching journals, field notes, and class histories. Through presenting our work at conferences and through writing articles and chapters, we were able to pull together what we had learned and see where we needed to continue our inquiry. Over the last three years we have reflected extensively, planned new inquiries, and taken action in our own settings. Writing this book has allowed us to reflect on what we understand about inquiry and classrooms and to identify the lingering questions that will continue to dominate our thinking as teachers.

Many of our lingering questions are related to issues we have discussed in this chapter. We want to understand more about sign systems and knowledge systems and how to integrate them into daily classroom life in a natural way, rather than as separate activities or times of the day. We struggle with getting past subject areas as the center of the curriculum. Everything in school seems to be organized around this belief. As we look at our schedules and classroom experiences, we still see how much subject areas continue to dominate our curriculum instead of serving as tools for inquiry.

We continue to have many questions about education for democracy. What does it look like in a classroom? How do we meaningfully involve students in behind-the-scenes decisions? Should students participate in all decision-making? How does education for democracy affect our roles as teachers? How do we practice democracy in a system that is traditionally a top-down hierarchy? Although we have learned a great deal about listening to our students, we continue to search for additional ways to highlight students' voices and stories.

We wonder about practical issues, such as what to do when students do not neatly divide themselves into five or six inquiry groups but have eight or nine questions that are important to them. Do we negotiate until there are only five or six sets of questions, or develop alternative organizational structures to support them in pursuing widely diverse questions? What is the relationship of personal inquiries to a class focus, and what are ways we can provide for both in our classrooms? We worry about students who are older, more knowledgeable, or domineering and who silence the voices of other children. We struggle with finding primary sources that are accessible for children.

We look at our busy (actually frantic) lives as educators and ask questions about the kinds of structures we need to keep growing and learning. Can these structures become part of school life, or will we always have to work at inquiry on our "own time" outside of our school and university contexts? We wonder about how to work at our relationships with teachers and educators in our school settings so that we can be supportive of their inquiries but also challenge and push our thinking with them.

We have made a lifelong commitment to inquiry. There are no easy solutions to our questions or to the dilemmas we face on a daily basis in our classrooms. We have created new understandings through our inquiry, but we know that there will always be other issues to consider. We are constantly alert to the tensions that will lead us to continue learning together through inquiry.

References

Professional Literature

Altwerger, B., and B. Flores. 1994. "Theme Cycles: Creating Communities of Learners." *Primary Voices K–6* 2, 1: 2–6.

Bang-Jensen, V. 1995. "Hands-on and First-hand Experiences in the Context of Reading and Language Arts." *Language Arts* 72: 352–58.

Barnes, D. 1976. *From Communication to Curriculum*. London: Penguin.

Bigelow, B. 1992. "Once upon a Genocide: Christopher Columbus in Children's Literature." *Language Arts* 69: 112–20.

Boyd, C. 1992. "Creating Curriculum from Children's Lives." *Primary Voices K–6* 1, 1: 22–27.

Burke, C. 1992. Presentation for LRC 696, Research in Language and Literacy. University of Arizona, Tucson.

Chase, P., and J. Doan. 1994. *Full Circle*. Portsmouth, NH: Heinemann.

Copeland, K. 1994. "Taking Down Roadblocks to Generative Learning." *Primary Voices K–6* 2, 3: 19–25.

Copenhaver, J. 1992. "Instances of Inquiry." *Primary Voices K–6* 1, 1: 6–12.

Crawford, K., M. Ferguson, G. Kauffman, J. Laird, J. Schroeder, and K. Short. 1994. "Exploring Historical and Multicultural Perspectives Through Inquiry." In *If This Is Social Studies, Why Isn't It Boring?* S. Steffey and W. Hood, eds. York, ME: Stenhouse.

Dewey, J. 1938. *Experience and Education*. New York: Collier.

Edelsky, C. 1994. "Education for Democracy." *Language Arts* 71, 1: 252–57.

Edmiston, B. 1993. "Going up the Beanstalk: Discovering Giant Possibilities for Responding to Literature Through Drama." In *Journeying: Children Responding to Literature*. K. Holland, R. Hungerford, and S. Ernst, eds. Portsmouth, NH: Heinemann.

Eisner, E. 1994. *Cognition and Curriculum Reconsidered*. New York: Teachers College Press.

Freire, P. 1985. *The Politics of Education*. South Hadley, MA: Bergin & Garvey.

Gagnon, P. 1988. "Why Study History?" *The Atlantic Monthly* (November): 43–66.

Goodman, K. 1967. "Reading: A Psycholinguistic Guessing Game." *Journal of the Reading Specialist* 4, 1: 126–35.

Goodman, Y. 1978. "Kidwatching: An Alternative to Testing." *Journal of National Elementary School Principals* 57, 4: 22–27.

Goodman, Y., and C. Burke. 1980. *Strategies in Reading: Focus on Comprehension*. New York: Holt.

Grant, C. 1977. "The Teacher and Multicultural Education: Some Personal Reflections." In *In Praise of Diversity: A Resource Book for Multicultural Education*. M. Gold, C. Grant, and H. Rivlin, eds. Washington, DC: Teacher Corps.

Graves, D. 1983. *Writing: Teachers and Children at Work*. Portsmouth, NH: Heinemann.

Harste, J. 1992. "Inquiry-Based Instruction." *Primary Voices K–6* 1, 1: 2–5.

Harste, J., K. Short, and C. Burke. 1988. *Creating Classrooms for Authors: The Reading-Writing Connection*. Portsmouth, NH: Heinemann.

Harste, J., V. Woodward, and C. Burke. 1984. *Language Stories and Literacy Lessons*. Portsmouth, NH: Heinemann.

Hornstein, S. 1994. "Towards a New Definition of Mathematical Literacy." Unpublished paper.

Kasten, W., and B. Clarke. 1993. *The Multi-age Classroom*. Katanah, NY: Richard C. Owen.

Kauffman, G., and K. Short. 1993. "Self-evaluation Portfolios: A Device to Empower Learners." In *Windows into Literacy: Assessing Learners K–8*. L. Rhodes and N. Shanklin, eds. Portsmouth, NH: Heinemann.

Kelly, P. 1990. "Guiding Young Students' Response to Literature. *The Reading Teacher* 43: 464–70.

Laird, J., and K. Crawford, with M. Ferguson, G. Kauffman, J. Schroeder, and K. Short. 1994. "Teachers as Collaborators for an Inquiry-based Curriculum." *Teacher Research* 1, 4: 111–21.

Levstik, L. 1987. "Exploring the Development of Historical Understanding." *Journal of Research and Development in Education* 21, 1: 1–15.

Lopez, B. 1992. *The Rediscovery of America*. New York: Random House.

O'Neill, C. 1982. *Drama Structures*. Portsmouth, NH: Heinemann.

Peterson, R. 1992. *Life in a Crowded Place*. Portsmouth, NH: Heinemann.

Piaget, J. 1977. *The Development of Thought*. New York: Viking.

Pierce, K. M., and C. Gilles, eds. 1993. *Cycles of Meaning: Exploring the Potential of Talk in Learning Communities*. Portsmouth, NH: Heinemann.

Pradl, G. 1996. "Reading and Democracy: The Enduring Influence of Louise Rosenblatt." *The New Advocate* 9, 1: 9–22.

Rethinking Schools. 1991. *Rethinking Columbus*. Milwaukee, WI: Rethinking Schools.

Rosen, H. 1984. *Stories and Meanings*. London: National Association for the Teaching of English.

Rowe, D. 1993. "Learning About Literacy and the World: Two-Year-Olds' and Teachers' Enactments of a Thematic Inquiry Curriculum." Paper presented at the National Reading Conference, Charleston, SC.

Ruiz, R. 1988. "Orientations in Language Planning." In *Language Diversity: Problem or Resource?* S. McKay and W. Wong, eds. New York: Newbury House.

Shannon, P. 1993. "Developing Democratic Voices." *The Reading Teacher* 47, 2: 86–94.

Shockley, B. 1993. "Extending the Literate Community: Reading and Writing with Families." *The New Advocate* 6, 1: 11–24.

Short, K. G. 1992. "Making Connections Across Literature and Life. In *Journeying: Children Responding to Literature*. K. Holland, R. Hungerford, and S. Ernst, eds. Portsmouth, NH: Heinemann.

————. 1993. "Curriculum for the 21st Century: A Redefinition." Speech given at the Annual Meeting of the National Council of Teachers of English, Pittsburgh, PA.

Short, K., and C. Burke. 1991. *Creating Curriculum*. Portsmouth, NH: Heinemann.

————. 1996. "Examining Our Beliefs and Practices Through Inquiry." *Language Arts* 73, 2: 97–104.

Short, K., with K. Crawford, M. Ferguson, G. Kauffman, J. Laird, and J. Schroeder. 1992. "A Critical Perspective on Discovery and Columbus: Exploring Children's Historical and Cultural Understandings." *Journal of Navajo Education* 10, 1: 6–16.

Short, K., and J. Harste, with C. Burke. 1996. *Creating Classrooms for Authors and Inquirers*. Portsmouth, NH: Heinemann.

Short, K., and K. M. Pierce, eds. 1990. *Talking About Books: Creating Literate Communities*. Portsmouth, NH: Heinemann.

Siegel, M. 1995. "More than Words: The Generative Power of Transmediations for Learning." *Canadian Journal of Education* 20, 4: 455–475.

Smith, K. 1990. "Entertaining a Text: A Reciprocal Process." In *Talking About Books: Creating Literate Communities*. K. Short and K. Pierce, eds. Portsmouth, NH: Heinemann.

————. 1992. Presentation for LRC 696, Research in Language and Literacy. University of Arizona, Tucson.

Taba, H. 1962. *Curriculum Development: Theory and Practice*. New York: Harcourt.

Upitis, R. 1990. *This Too Is Music*. Portsmouth, NH: Heinemann.

Vygotsky, L. 1978. *Mind in Society*. Cambridge, MA: Harvard University Press.

Watson, D., C. Burke, and J. Harste. 1989. *Inquiring Voices*. New York: Scholastic.

Whitin, D., H. Mills, and T. O'Keefe. 1990. *Living and Learning Mathematics*. Portsmouth, NH: Heinemann.

Children's Literature

Aardema, V. 1991. *Borreguita and the Coyote: A Tale from Ayulta, Mexico*. Illus. P. Mathers. New York: Knopf.

Adler, D. 1991. *A Picture Book of Christopher Columbus*. Illus. J. and A. Wallner. New York: Holiday.

Aliki. 1965. *A Weed Is a Flower: The Life of George Washington Carver*. New York: Prentice Hall.

———. 1976. *Corn Is Maize: The Gift of the Indians*. New York: HarperCollins.

Andrews, J. 1985. *Very Last First Time*. Illus. I. Wallace. New York: Atheneum.

———. 1991. *The Auction*. Illus. K. Reczuch. New York: Macmillan.

Asimov, I. 1974. *How Did We Find Out About Germs?* New York: Avon.

Babbitt, N. 1975. *Tuck Everlasting*. New York: Trumpet.

Baker, J. 1988. *Where the Forest Meets the Sea*. New York: Greenwillow.

———. 1991. *Window*. New York: Greenwillow.

Banks, L. R. 1981. *The Indian in the Cupboard*. New York: Doubleday.

Barchas, S. 1975. *I Was Walking Down the Road*. Illus. J. Kent. New York: Scholastic.

Batherman, M. 1981. *Before Columbus*. Boston: Houghton Mifflin.

Begaye, L. S. 1993. *Building a Bridge*. Illus. L. Tracy. Flagstaff, AZ: Northland.

Bellows, C. 1987. *Four Fat Rats*. New York: Macmillan.

Blood, C., and M. Link. 1976. *The Goat in the Rug*. Illus. N. Parker. New York: Four Winds.

Bradman, T. 1989. *The Sandal*. Illus. P. DuPasquier. New York: Viking.

Brown, M., and C. Perrault. 1954. *Cinderella*. New York: Scribner.

Buckley, C. 1984. *Greedy Gray Octopus*. Illus. D. Pearson. Crystal Lake, IL: Rigby.

Bunting, E. 1988. *How Many Days to America? A Thanksgiving Story*. Illus. B. Peck. New York: Clarion.

———. 1992. *Summer Wheels*. Illus. T. Allen. San Diego: Harcourt.

Burnett, F. 1938. *The Secret Garden*. Illus. N. Unwin. Philadelphia: Lippincott.

Byars, B. 1977. *The Pinballs*. New York: Scholastic.

Caduto, M., and J. Bruchac. 1989. *Keepers of the Earth: Native American Stories and Wildlife Activities for Children*. Golden, CO: Fulcrum.

Carlson, N. 1988. *I Like Me!* New York: Viking.

Carryl, C. 1992. *The Walloping Window-Blind*. Illus. T. Rand. New York: Arcade.

Cherry, L. 1992. *A River Ran Wild*. San Diego: Harcourt.

Coerr, E. 1977. *Sadako and the Thousand Paper Cranes*. New York: Putnam.

Conrad, P. 1991. *Pedro's Journal: A Voyage with Christopher Columbus*. Honesdale, PA: Boyds Mills Press.

Cooney, B. 1982. *Miss Rumphius*. New York: Viking.

Crowder, J., and F. Hill. 1986. *Tonibah and the Rainbow*. Bernalillo, NM: Upper Strata Ink.

De Brunhoff, J. 1933. *The Story of Babar, the Little Elephant*. New York: Random House.

Dorris, M. 1992. *Morning Girl*. New York: Hyperion.

Durell, A., and M. Sachs, eds. 1990. *The Big Book for Peace*. New York: Dutton.

Ekoomiak, N. 1990. *Arctic Memories*. New York: Holt.

Esbensen, B. 1992. *Who Shrank My Grandmother's House? Poems of Discovery*. Illus. E. Beddows. New York: HarperCollins.

Fischetto, L. 1991. *All Pigs on Deck: Christopher Columbus's Second Marvelous Voyage*. Illus. L. Galli. New York: Delacorte.

Fisher, L. E. 1990. *Prince Henry the Navigator*. New York: Macmillan.

Floethe, L. 1956. *The Winning Colt*. Illus. R. Floethe. New York: Sterling.

Foreman, M. 1991. *The Boy Who Sailed with Columbus*. New York: Archade.

Franklin, K. 1992. *The Old, Old Man and the Very Little Boy*. Illus. T. Shaffer. New York: Atheneum.

Fritz, J. 1980. *Where Do You Think You're Going, Christopher Columbus?* New York: Putnam.

———. 1992. *The World in 1492*. New York: Holt.

Galbraith, K. 1990. *Laura Charlotte*. Illus. F. Cooper. New York: Philomel.

Garcia, M. 1986. *The Adventures of Connie and Diego*. Illus. I. M. Montoya. Emeryville, CA: Children's Book Press.

Garza, C. 1990. *Family Pictures*. Emeryville, CA: Children's Book Press.

Gerrard, R. 1988. *Sir Francis Drake: His Daring Deeds*. New York: Farrar Straus Giroux.

Gilman, P. 1994. *Something from Nothing*. New York: Scholastic.

Ginsburg, M. 1976. *Two Greedy Bears*. New York: Macmillan.

Gleiter, J., and K. Thompson. 1985. *Christopher Columbus*. Nashville, TN: Ideals.

Goble, P. 1988. *Iktomi and the Boulder: A Plains Indian Story*. New York: Orchard.

Goode, D. 1991. *Where's Our Mama?* New York: Dutton.

Gray, N. 1989. *A Country Far Way*. New York: Orchard.

Guarino, D. 1989. *Is Your Mama a Llama?* Illus. S. Kellogg. New York: Scholastic.

Harper, A. 1986. *It's not Fair!* Illus. S. Hellard. New York: Putnam.

Hartman, G. 1991. *As the Crow Flies: A First Book of Maps*. Illus. H. Stevenson. New York: Bradbury.

Haskins, J. 1991. *Outward Dreams: Black Inventors and Their Inventions*. New York: Walker.

Havill, J. 1986. *Jamaica's Find*. Illus. A. S. O'Brien. New York: Scholastic.

Hayes, J. 1983. *Coyote &: Native American Folktales*. Santa Fe, NM: Mariposa.

Hopkins L. B., and M. Arenstein. 1990. *Do You Know What Day Tommorrow Is?* New York: Scholastic.

Houston, G. 1992. *My Great-Aunt Arizona*. Illus. S. Lamb. New York: HarperCollins.

Howard, E. 1991. *Aunt Flossie's Hats (and Crabcakes Later)*. Illus. J. Ransome. New York: Clarion.

Hutchins, P. 1968. *Rosie's Walk*. New York: Greenwillow.

References

Ikeda, D. 1992. *Over the Deep Blue Sea*. Illus. B. Wildsmith. New York: Knopf.

Jacobs, F. 1992. *The Tainos: The People Who Welcomed Columbus*. New York: Putnam.

Jeffers, S. 1991. *Brother Eagle, Sister Sky: A Message from Chief Seattle*. New York: Dial.

Johnston, T. 1988. *Yonder*. Illus. L. Bloom. New York: Puffin.

Keegan, M. 1991. *Pueblo Boy: Growing Up in Two Worlds*. New York: Cobblehill.

Kellogg, S. 1973. *Island of the Skog*. New York: Dial.

———. 1986. *Best Friends*. New York: Dial.

Krensky, S. 1991. *Children of the Earth and Sky: Five Stories About Native American Children*. New York: Scholastic.

Lacapa, M., and K. Lacapa. 1994. *Less Than Half, More Than Whole*. Flagstaff, AZ: Northland.

Lattimore, D. 1987. *The Flame of Peace: A Tale of the Aztecs*. New York: HarperCollins.

Lauber, P. 1990. *Seeing Earth from Space*. New York: Macmillan.

L'Hommedieu, D. 1955. *Pompon*. Illus. M. Nichols. New York: Farrar, Straus, Giroux.

Liestman, V. 1991. *Columbus Day*. Minneapolis, MN: Carolrhoda.

Littledale, F. 1966. *The Magic Fish*. Illus. W. P. Pels. New York: Scholastic.

Locker, T. 1991. *The Land of Gray Wolf*. New York: Dial.

Lowry, L. 1989. *Number the Stars*. New York: Dell.

Lyon, G. E. 1990. *Basket*. Illus. M. Szilagyi. New York: Orchard.

———. 1992. *Who Came Down That Road*. Illus. P. Catalanotto. New York: Orchard.

Maestro, B., and G. Maestro. 1991. *The Discovery of the Americas*. New York: Lothrop.

Matthews, R. 1991. *Eyewitness: Explorer*. New York: Knopf.

McGill-Callahan, S. 1991. *And Still the Turtle Watched*. Illus. B. Moser. New York: Dial.

McLerran, A. 1991. *Roxaboxen*. Illus. B. Cooney. New York: Lothrop.

Meltzer, M. 1990. *Columbus and the World Around Him*. New York: Watts.

Merriam, E. 1991. *The Wise Woman and Her Secret*. Illus. L. Graves. New York: Simon & Schuster.

Morris, A. 1989. *Bread Bread Bread*. New York: Lothrop.

Naidoo, B. 1986. *Journey to Jo'burg: A South African Story*. New York: HarperCollins.

Naylor, P. 1973. *To Walk the Sky Path*. New York: Dell.

———. 1991. *Shiloh*. New York: Dell.

New Mexico People & Energy Collective. 1981. *Red Ribbons for Emma*. Berkeley, CA: New Seed Press.

Nobisso, J. 1990. *Grandma's Scrapbook*. Illus. M. Hyde. San Marcos, CA: Green Tiger Press.

Obrist, J. 1984. *The Miser Who Wanted the Sun*. New York: Atheneum.

Ortiz, S. 1977. *The People Shall Continue*. Emeryville, CA: Children's Book Press.

Parker, S. 1992. *Galileo and the Universe*. New York: HarperCollins.

Paulson, T. 1990. *Jack and the Beanstalk and the Beanstalk Incident*. New York: Birch Lane.

Paterson, K. 1977. *Bridge to Terabithia*. New York: Dell.

Pelta, K. 1991. *Discovering Christopher Columbus: How History Is Invented*. Minneapolis, MN: Lerner.

Polacco, P. 1988. *The Keeping Quilt*. New York: Simon & Schuster.

_____. 1990. *Babushka's Doll*. New York: Simon & Schuster.

_____. 1992. *Mrs. Katz and Tush*. New York: Bantam.

Potter, B. 1987. *The Tale of Peter Rabbit*. New York: Viking.

Precek, K. 1989. *A Penny in the Road*. Illus. P. Cullen-Clark. New York: Macmillan.

Provensen, A., and M. Provensen. 1983. *The Glorious Flight Across the Channel with Louis Bleriot, July 25, 1909*. New York: Viking.

Pryor, B. 1992. *The House on Maple Street*. Illus. B. Peck. New York: Morrow.

Ride, S., and S. Oakie. 1987. *To Space and Back*. New York: Lothrop.

Rodanas, K. 1991. *Dragonfly's Tale*. New York: Clarion.

Rogers, P. 1987. *From Me to You*. Illus. J. Johnson. New York: Orchard.

Roop, P., and C. Roop, eds. 1991. *I, Columbus: My Journal–1492*. New York: Avon.

Rose, D. 1990. *The People Who Hugged the Trees*. Illus. B. Saflund. Niwot, CO: Roberts Rhinehart.

Ryan, P. 1990. *Explorers and Mapmakers*. New York: Lodestar.

Rylant, C. 1986. *A Fine White Dust*. New York: Bradbury.

_____. 1987. *Birthday Presents*. Illus. S. Stevenson. New York: Orchard.

Say, A. 1990. *El Chino*. Boston: Houghton Mifflin.

Scholes, K. 1989. *Peace Begins with You*. Illus. R. Ingpen. Boston: Little, Brown.

Schroeder, A. 1995. *Carolina Shout!* Illus. B. Fuchs. New York: Dial.

Scieszka, J. 1989. *The True Story of the Three Little Pigs*. Illus. L. Smith. New York: Orchard.

Scott, A. H. 1990. *Grandmother's Chair*. Illus. M. Aubrey. New York: Clarion.

Seuss, Dr. 1938. *The 500 Hats of Bartholomew Cubbins*. New York: Random House.

_____. 1957. *How the Grinch Stole Christmas*. New York: Random House.

Sharmat, M. 1980. *Gila Monsters Meet You at the Airport*. New York: Aladdin.

Sierra, J., and R. Kaminski. 1976. "The Elegant Rooster." In *Multicultural Folktales: Stories to Tell Young Children*. Phoenix, AZ: Oryx Press.

Sis, P. 1991. *Follow the Dream*. New York: Knopf.

Slobodkina, E. 1940. *Caps for Sale*. Reading, MA: Addison-Wesley.

Spier, P. 1980. *People*. New York: Doubleday.

Stanley, D., and P. Vennema. 1994. *Cleopatra*. Illus. D. Stanley. New York: Morrow.

Sullivan, G. 1990. *The Day We Walked on the Moon*. New York: Scholastic.

Surat, M. 1983. *Angel Child, Dragon Child*. Illus. V. Mai. New York: Scholastic.

References

Taylor, M. 1976. *Roll of Thunder, Hear My Cry*. New York: Viking.

———. 1981. *Song of the Trees*. New York: Bantam.

———. 1987. *The Friendship and the Gold Cadillac*. New York: Bantam.

———. 1990. *Mississippi Bridge*. New York: Bantam.

Temple, F. 1993. *Grab Hands and Run*. New York: Orchard.

Thompson, K. 1955. *Eloise*. New York: Simon & Schuster.

Turner, A. 1987. *Nettie's Trip South*. Illus. R. Himler. New York: Macmillan.

Waddell, M. 1989. *Once There Were Giants*. New York: Delacorte.

———. 1990. *Grandma's Bill*. New York: Orchard.

Walsh, J. P. 1982. *The Green Book*. New York: Farrar, Strauss, Giroux.

———. 1992. *When Grandma Came*. Illus. S. Williams. New York: Viking.

Warner, L. S. 1993. *From Slave to Abolitionist: The Life of William Wells Brown*. New York: Dial.

Weaver, L. 1993. *Close to Home: A Story of the Polio Epidemic*. Illus. A. Arrington. New York: Viking.

Weiss, H. 1991. *Maps: Getting from Here to There*. Boston: Houghton Mifflin.

Wheatley, N. 1987. *My Place*. Illus. D. Rawlins. Melbourne, Australia: Collins Dove.

Willard, N. 1987. *The Voyage of the Ludgate Hill: A Journey with Robert Louis Stevenson*. Illus. A. and M. Provensen. San Diego: Harcourt.

Williams, B. 1975. *Kevin's Grandmother*. Illus. K. Chorao. New York: Dutton.

Williams, J. 1976. *Everyone Knows What a Dragon Looks Like*. Illus. M. Mayer. New York: Four Winds.

Williams, V. 1981. *Three Days on a River in a Red Canoe*. New York: Mulberry.

Winter, J. 1988. *Follow the Drinking Gourd*. New York: Knopf.

Wood, A. 1982. *Quick as a Cricket*. Illus. D. Wood. Lewiston, ME: Child's Play.

Yashima, T. 1955. *Crow Boy*. New York: Viking.

Yee, P. 1991. *Roses Sing on New Snow: A Delicious Tale*. New York: Macmillian.

Yep, L. 1975. *Dragonwings*. New York: HarperCollins.

Yolen, J. 1977. *The Seeing Stick*. Illus. E. Young. New York: Crowell.

———. 1988. *The Devil's Arithmetic*. New York: Viking.

———. 1990. *Sky Dogs*. Illus. B. Moser. San Diego: Harcourt.

———. 1992. *Encounter*. Illus. D. Shannon. San Diego: Harcourt.

Yorinks, A. 1987. *Company's Coming*. Illus. R. Egielski. New York: Scholastic.

Young, E. 1992. *Seven Blind Mice*. New York: Philomel.

Yue, C., and D. Yue. 1992. *Christopher Columbus: How He Did It*. Boston: Houghton Mifflin.

Zelinksy, P. 1992. *Rumpelstiltskin*. New York: Dutton.

Zolotow, C. 1972. *William's Doll*. Illus. W. Pene du Bois. New York: Harper-Collins.

———. 1992. *This Quiet Lady*. Illus. A. Lobel. New York: Greenwillow.